SALLY MORGAN ENTERTAINMENTS

My Heavenly Truth

My Heavenly Truth

Connections to the Afterlife

SALLY MORGAN

SALLY MORGAN ENTERTAINMENTS

SALLY MORGAN ENTERTAINMENTS LTD

Published by Sally Morgan Entertainments Ltd

Sally Morgan Entertainments Ltd, Reigate Business Centre,
7-11 High Street, Reigate, RH2 9AA

Sally Morgan Entertainments Ltd, Registered Offices: Argyll House,
23 Brook Street, Kingston-Upon-Thames, Surrey, KT1 2BN

www.sallymorgan.tv

First published 2013

Set in 12.5/14.75pt Garamond MT Std
Typeset in England by CPI Typesetting
Printed and bound by CPI Group (UK) Ltd, Croydon, CR0 4YY

Some names, locations and details have been changed to
protect the identities and privacy of the individuals involved

2 4 6 8 9 7 5 3

ISBN: 978-0-9927001-0-2

Contents

This book is dedicated to my darlings Rebecca and Fern. Thank you from the bottom of my heart for your continual support and understanding. You may have a mum who is physically absent when I am out on the road, but I am always there in your hearts.

Prologue
London: June, 2013

The court room was much smaller than I had expected. The hard wooden benches were set out in formal rows like pews in a church. They faced forward and were sloped towards the judge's chair, giving the spectators a view of the raised seat where the decisions were made. The walls around the side of the chamber were lined with dark oak-panelling and book shelves which heaved under the weight of hundreds of thick leather-bound tomes. The general impression was a cross between *Hogwarts* and *Rumpole of the Bailey.* The atmosphere was sombre, almost oppressive. The weight of history and authority bore down on the rows of people seated in the room. The musty smell added to the serious ambience. It was the sort of place that made you whisper and my psychic antenna was twitching. I could feel the energy seeping from the walls. All the emotions had permeated the air in that space over hundreds of years; the jubilation and the disappointments.

I looked around me. I was surrounded by scores of friends and family; my supporters and loved ones. They were waiting quietly in anticipation, speaking occasionally in hushed voices. Every now and then someone would catch my eye and give me an encouraging smile or a wink.

I was in the Royal Courts of Justice in London and I was a bag of nerves. Moments before I had been laughing and chatting in a cafe across the road with 'Team Sally', which included my husband John, my daughters Fern and Rebecca, staff from my office and my legal team. My mood changed as soon as I crossed the busy street and saw the imposing historic building. As we walked through the airport-style security check at the front and into the grand stone-vaulted entrance hall, the chatter and laughter became hushed. My stomach started to turn cartwheels.

The High Court, as it is also known, marked the end of long, hard journey. It was the final destination in a nightmare that had started 18 months before. I was there for vindication after being accused of cheating by a national newspaper. I could have walked away from the claim that had been made against me but I refused and took the decision to clear my name. In reality I had no choice. The accusation was unjustified and unfair and I could not just stand there and let it go unacknowledged. Out of principle I needed to let the world, and most importantly my fans and the people I had helped over the years, know that I had done nothing wrong and that I was not a cheat.

In the court room the black-robed judge took his seat. John sat next to me and squeezed my hand. I smiled back at him. My heart was pounding in my chest. The judge began to read out the statement that would finally vindicate me.

The nightmare had started many months earlier. I remember it as clearly as if it was yesterday. It is etched on my memory. It was the day my life appeared to crumble around me and there was nothing I could do to prevent it.

It was September and I was preparing to throw a party for family and friends to celebrate my birthday. I woke up buzzing with anticipation and was looking forward to the events ahead. I lay in bed for a few minutes enjoying the silence outside and made a mental checklist in my head. Did we have enough food and drink? Would I need to get a few more chairs? Would the marquee arrive on time? We had invited around 100 people and several were travelling from abroad. I hadn't seen them for years and was excited about catching up with them and hearing their news. It was going to be a good night. John was asleep beside me, mouth agape, snoring loudly. I nudged him awake. He had his chores to do and I wanted to make sure he did them in good time.

I have always loved throwing parties. I love to entertain, which is just as well given what I do for a living! I am not extravagant or a show-off, but I like to host a good bash and love to watch my family and friends enjoying themselves. The party was going to give me an opportunity to say thank you to everyone for the love and support they had given me through the years. It was also going to give me the opportunity to wear the new dress I'd bought from a boutique in London for the occasion; another reason I was excited about the coming festivities.

It had been a busy year up until that day. Apart from a few weeks break in the summer I had been touring non-stop. I'd performed in venues across the length and breadth of the UK, from the West Country to Scotland and Ireland. And it was at one of my shows in Ireland where, unbeknown to me, the trouble had started.

The first I heard about it was through a call from my office. I'd just got out of bed when the phone rang. I lifted the receiver. Hayley, my hard-working artist manager, was on the other end of the line.

'Please don't worry Sally,' she began, 'there is a story in the Daily Mail today that you will need to have a look at.'

She went on to explain the content of the article. A few days after one of my shows in Dublin an Irish radio station was holding a phone-in and two anonymous women called to allege that they had sat at the back of the auditorium and had heard voices coming from a room behind them where the sound and lighting technicians were working. They falsely believed that someone in the room was communicating information to me. The inference was that somehow information had been gleaned from members of the audience prior to the show and was then being broadcast to me secretly so I could use it in the show. Basically I was being called a cheat. It was preposterous theory. To stage such an operation in every show I had done over the years would have been impossible. But I had become used to people trying to work out 'how I did it'. There will always be doubters who can't get their heads around what I do. The irony of course is that I have always been honest about what I do. I really do communicate with spirit; I am a medium and have been since I can remember. Nevertheless the sceptics and people who cannot bring themselves to believe in an afterlife assume I am indulged in some form of trickery.

The newspaper reported on the content of this phone-in show. No one had contacted the women and no one had contacted me or my office to put the allegations to me and allow me to refute them, which was unfair and, as far as I was concerned, contrary to the principals of balanced journalism.

I finished the phone call with Hayley and put the receiver down. I had a sick feeling in my stomach. I felt crestfallen; the air had been knocked out of me. I had been working as a medium for long enough to realise the implications of such a serious allegation. And more than anything I felt sad for my family and my fans. My loved ones would have to face the barrage of questions that such an accusation would inevitably invite and my fans would be left with doubt. The most important facet of what I do is the three-way triangle of trust between spirit, my fans and me. Without that mutual trusting bond, the process would not work. Spirit would not come through and I would not be able to pass on messages. Anything that chipped away at that unique interplay and put barriers up in the process could not be good.

The more I thought about what was being alleged, the sadder I got. Soon after, the phone calls started as more people read the story. I tried to put a brave face on things but it was hard.

It's a load of rubbish,' I told people. 'There is no truth to it at all.'

Along with the sadness, I started to feel a growing sense of anger at the injustice of what had been written. There was no proof, it was lies.

The party came and went and, if I am honest, I was glad when the day was over. For me it had been ruined. All day long I was fighting back waves of emotion. My team and I then set about defending my reputation. We contacted the theatre where the allegation had originated from. They were equally upset as by association the piece implied that they were also being dishonest. I issued a statement categorically denying the claim, as did the theatre. I also pointed out that the members of staff who were supposed to be feeding me information were in fact sub-contracted by the theatre and so not part of my on-the-road team at all. Surely if I had been conducting such a well-thought-out and complicated con I would have entrusted the execution of it to my own staff, rather than casual workers I did not know and had no links with.

In the face of these facts I mistakenly thought that would be the end of it and my team requested that the newspaper remove the allegation from their website and apologise. It seemed like a logical and fair course of action.

But unfortunately that was not the end of it. Two days later the same paper printed another story; a follow-up to the original piece. This time it was written by a well-known sceptic, the magician Paul Zenon. In the piece he discussed his views on psychics and the allegation made against me was repeated.

By this time the story had spread. It was being discussed on television programmes and on radio shows. My phone was ringing off the hook. Journalists from all over the world were calling to speak to me. No matter how much I defended myself I was not being heard.

I began to get abusive messages through my website and on Twitter. I was accused of taking advantage of the bereaved and vulnerable. There were death threats. I felt terrified and besieged. I have never felt so helpless in my life. I didn't know what to do.

In the following months there were many low points. Several weeks after the stories were published, as the repercussions rumbled on, I received a letter which broke my heart. It was from a client of mine from back in the days before I started touring and had run a successful practice from home. I had helped her through some very dark years following the death of her husband and we had formed a bond which crossed over from a professional relationship to one of friendship. I had told her so many things that I could not possibly have known without the ability to contact spirit world and she trusted in my ability. I had given her hope. The letter she sent called all that into doubt.

'I am so sad to read that it was all a trick Sally,' she wrote. 'I trusted you and I feel betrayed.' I felt numb as I read her words. My heart went out to her and I wanted to hug her and tell her it was a lie and that I would never, ever cheat the people who came to me.

I knew that for her, for my family and for all the hundreds of thousands of people who had paid to come and see me over the previous years I had no choice but to launch a legal case to clear my name. I had been libelled and I needed to rectify that. I was not naive. I knew it would be costly and that it would not be easy. I called my lawyer, Graham Atkins, with a heavy heart. I felt backed into a corner. I did not do it to be a spokesperson for mediums and mediumship or for financial gain. I had done nothing wrong and deserved to have that acknowledged. I had never cheated.

There will always be sceptics who attack my work and I understood and accepted that. However, to libel me by falsely accusing me of a con trick did not constitute rational commentary or debate.

The wheels of justice seemed to turn incredibly slowly. It took well over a year to get to the stage where I received the vindication I deserved. During that time I felt I was living under a cloud. I had some very dark days indeed.

There were times when I felt so down and depressed that I couldn't even get out of bed. I would lie there numbly, trying to muster the energy to face another day. Dark thoughts would swirl around my head. What had I done to deserve it all? I started to think long and hard about my life. As far as I was concerned the accusation that had been made did not just cover that one incident, it called into question my whole life. I had been experiencing psychic events all my life and so, if the article alleged that I cheated at that specific show, the inference was that I had been lying all my life.

I recalled some of the countless incidents from my past which could not be explained by any trickery. At eight-years-old I told one of my teachers that I knew he had thrown crockery at his wife that morning. He had. How did I know that? Was I cheating then? Of course I wasn't. How did I know the names of the dead relatives of the people I was talking to even when I was teenager? There were no computers to research people on or hidden earpieces then. In the early days of my practice at home there was no Google or Facebook. I couldn't check the social media profiles of the people that were coming to see me. Half the time before they arrived all I knew about them was their Christian names. But somehow once they sat with me I managed to know intimate details about their lives. The details just appeared as thought patterns in my head. I ran a practice from home for over 40 years. If it was all a con how was I doing it? And my practice was built up on reputation and recommendation, I never needed to advertise. Surely through all those years, if I was anything other than genuine I would have been found out. It defied logic.

I thought about some of the many funny times I'd had and some of the Eureka moments when people's doubts had been swept aside by my accuracy.

Years ago I used to do readings for small gatherings in community halls and afterwards I would come off the stage and talk to the people. One night I had given a woman an incredible message and she came up to me after the show to talk. She was standing with her husband who wore a trilby hat. He reminded me of my grandfather. She was dressed in a long frock and had flyaway hair and heavily rouged cheeks. She looked like a proper eccentric.

'I don't know how you know all that stuff but I still don't believe it,' she said bluntly. 'I still think there is some kind of trickery.'

Even back then I was used to people questioning my ability. I guess if I wasn't a medium and someone was doing what I was doing, I would wonder how they did it too.

'I am not asking you to believe,' I shrugged. 'But what I said to you was correct wasn't it?'

She acknowledged that the details I had given were indeed correct.

'I don't know how you knew it all,' she repeated. Neither did I.

'But if you were to tell me what colour knickers I have on, I'd believe you,' she laughed.

'They are red,' I told her. She was flabbergasted and there, in the middle of the crowd of people, she pulled up her skirt and showed me her red drawers. 'I believe, I believe,' she repeated, laughing.

When she had calmed down I spoke to her.

'Knowing what colour knickers you are wearing could have been a lucky guess,' I acknowledged. 'So why did you believe me when I might have guessed something but you didn't believe me when I was genuinely picking up accurate information that was so specific I couldn't of guessed it?'

It was a good point and one I have tried to make throughout my life. By all means judge me on what I do, but the benchmark should be my accuracy, not supposition and unfounded allegation. Unfortunately the memo had not got through to the people at the newspaper when those articles were written and the months rumbled on slowly as my legal team worked hard to get an apology and to clear my name. All the time my friends and family had to endure constant remarks from people. At best they had to bat back questions about the claims, at worst they had to endure taunts and abuse. It was their support and the support and strength I got from my fans which kept me going and which ultimately kept me sane.

The first six months were the worst. At one point I seriously considered giving it all up and leaving the country. It was one night after a show. I was with John and we were heading home in the car.

'You're quiet,' he said to me. 'What's troubling you?'

As ever the show had been a success but the magic events on stage only held off the black feeling which returned when I was on my own and at the mercy of my own thoughts. I turned to him.

'I think I've had enough of it all John,' I sighed. 'I don't know if I can carry on doing this. I am tired.'

'What do you mean,' he asked. 'Tired of what?'

'I'm tired of having to defend myself and feeling like I am living under in cloud. Our lives are in limbo while all this is going on. I just want it to end or to go away. I think we should sell up and move away. Start again somewhere else; emigrate.'

The roles of our relationship had reversed. I was always the positive one. My glass was always half full. John, on the other hand, was usually Mr Doom and Gloom. If there was a negative to be had from a situation John would find it. It's why we work so well together. He is the yin to my yang! In this instance he gave me a pep talk.

'You can't think like that Sally. What has happened is unfair and it is all lies, we know that and the rest of the world will know that too. If you leave now and give up, some people will take that as a sign that the story is true. We have no choice but to see this thing through, get justice and be strong. We have nothing to hide. Things will get better, I promise.'

I had even started to change the way I behaved

on stage. I did not realise it at first. One of the crew pointed it out.

'Every time you start talking to someone who has stood to take a message you ask them to confirm that you have never met before.' He was right. I caught myself doing it again and again.

'I don't know you do I?' I asked repeatedly at every show. 'There is no way I could have known what I have just told you, is there?'

I double-checked myself all the time. I was so aware that people in the audience may have read the stories or that there could be people in the audience who had bought tickets with the sole aim of catching me out that I was constantly letting them know there was no trickery involved. It felt like I was walking on eggshells. Thankfully my ability never left me and I continued to work as I had always done; with faith and belief. And because of that, spirit never deserted me.

Finally, in June 2013 I found myself sitting in the Royal Courts of Justice ready to hear the words I had been waiting all that time to hear.

Graham was dressed in his black robes and looked very serious when he stood and began reading the statement that had been agreed by the legal team representing the newspaper.

'Mrs Morgan is a psychic. In the last five years or so, she has become well-known through appearing on television and through her theatre shows around the country in which she performs to large audiences. She has performed in over 600 shows in more than 100 different theatres or venues, to audiences stretching into the hundreds of thousands.'

He went on to explain the basis of why I was suing the newspaper for libel. I clung on to every word.

'The allegation contained in the article that Mrs Morgan cheated the audience in Dublin is completely false and defamatory of her. It has also caused enormous distress to Mrs Morgan, who decided, given the newspaper's initial defence of the article, that she had no choice but to commence legal proceedings against the publisher of the Daily Mail. I am pleased to say that the Daily Mail has now accepted that the allegation is untrue and is here by its solicitor today to apologise for the publication of the allegation. It has also agreed to pay Mrs Morgan substantial damages together with her legal costs.'

Then the newspaper's solicitor stood to make her statement.

'The Daily Mail withdraws the suggestion that Mrs Morgan used a secret earpiece at her Dublin show in September 2011 to receive messages from off-stage, thereby cheating her audience, which it accepts is untrue.'

I felt the weight of the last months begin to lift from my shoulders.

The lady continued.

'It apologises unreservedly to Mrs Morgan for publishing the allegation.'

Words had never sounded sweeter. It had been a

long, hard battle and costly both in terms of finance and emotions. Even my health had deteriorated in the difficult months. I was so preoccupied with the troubles I faced that on many occasions I would skip meals and as, several years ago I underwent gastric surgery which meant that I had to be very careful about what I ate, my diet and wellbeing suffered.

The days following the court appearance were a blur. I received many requests for interviews. The television shows that had shunned me after the allegation wanted me to be a guest. I refused. I spoke to a few select, supportive publications. I was not out for revenge and I did not feel jubilant. I felt vindicated and as long as people realised that what I did was genuine, I was happy.

A month after the apology I set off for a tour of Australia, happy in the knowledge that my reputation had been restored.

It is hard to draw positives from the whole experience but as I mentioned previously, I am naturally an upbeat person and there has been one overriding plus-point to come from the whole tale. What I do – my psychic ability – was called into question in such a fundamental way that I started to really think about the gift I have. I never doubted my ability but, as questions were being asked of me, so I started to ask questions about myself. What was really happening each night when I stood before an audience and started to relay messages to them? What were the strange and magical mechanisms which allowed those amazing things to happen? How did it work? What were messages made of? Where did they come from and why was I able to hear, smell and feel them?

I became fascinated by the psychic process more than I ever had. I looked for patterns and clues; anything that would provide some indication about the how and the why. I had always thought about what I did and had never taken the gift I have for granted but I wanted to learn more deeply.

Over the years so many people have asked me what goes on inside my head and I wanted to know too. I wanted to look at psychic ability in an analytical way and to try and formulate some kind of theory for what happens. I've often been challenged by sceptics to undergo scientific testing to prove myself. I don't need to because the proof is there each night I host a show. Instead I started to analyse myself.

I think I knew when I started the process of inquiry that I would probably never find absolute answers; after all, we are dealing with the most fundamental human question of all here! What really does happen to us after we die?

At some stages along this journey of self-discovery I was beset by personal fear. I worried that if I really looked too hard and started to discover what was happening I would upset some form of natural balance and my ability would be taken away, or it would frighten me so much that I would run away from it. It's as deep as you can get. Sometimes it felt like poking a hornet's nest. I worried that I would get stung.

I'm not able to use scientific experience as I am not an academic. The only test I ever passed in life was my driving test and I didn't pass that the first time! But I am curious, I always have been and curiosity drives understanding. Without curiosity we would never learn.

In the midst of my despair I set out to question everything and to find the kernels of truth about what it means to be a medium and how it all works. That is what this book is about; questions about life and death from a psychic perspective. I have written it in two parts. The first part sets out my ideas and theories about the whole psychic process. I have used observations made during the shows I have performed to try to understand what happens when 1000 people sit in a room and open themselves up to the possibility of an afterlife. The results are often amazing.

In the second part of this book I set out to answer the most common questions I get asked about spirit, mediumship, life and death. Again I use examples from my work to illustrate my ideas.

I hope that by trying to decipher the wonderful things I experience and by answering these questions I can bring you closer to spirit world.

PART ONE
Energy

Psychic awakening: message building

The audience had settled into their seats. The show was a sell-out. It was one of the coldest nights on record in the north of England and outside in the streets freshly fallen snow was beginning to carpet the road. Despite the weather over 1000 people had turned out to see me and, as ever, I was grateful to them. I marvelled at the trust they showed in me and thanked them quietly from the wings. None of us knew how the night would pan out. There was no script. I had not planned anything. Apart from the regular features such as the love letters people left and the photographs they gave me to read from, nothing was for certain. But I knew it was going to be dynamite. It always was. I trusted in the process and spirit world always delivered.

Hours before the show the indications that we were in for a good night had began. The messages had started to come through. It began with flashes of images in my mind; faces, scenes, places and objects. Then the voices started. They told me their names, their addresses, the names of their loved ones. They told me things about themselves and showed me their final moments. Anyone else experiencing these often unsettling thoughts, internal sounds and feelings would probably think they were going mad. It appeared to be a random stream of unconnected unconscious brain babble! But I knew it wasn't. It was proof to me that the mysterious ability that had been with me all my life was alive inside me and was working well. The messages I received were from what I term 'spirit world' which was cranking itself up, ready to make the connection with the living world that I would facilitate later that evening. The mental images and feelings were not the same as the data and information we take in as we make our way through life. Together they were an energy, they grew, changed form, got louder and quieter; there was something organic about the process. The details that were slotting into my mind were not my thoughts. Although to some extent I could mediate the process and channel the energy through my mind almost like a filter, I could not affect the content of the information.

I stood by the side of the stage waiting for the introduction to end with all this going on inside my head. It felt like my brain was being filled up like the petrol tank of a car. The music climaxed and I made my big entrance. By that time the energy had crystallised into images in my mind so clear I felt I could touch them. I was surrounded by people only I could see, they were speaking to me. Some were excitedly pointing out people in the audience. Some were calling out names. Others were quietly standing in the shadows waiting their turn.

If I'd have had some kind of magical psychic

x-ray specs I would have been able to see arcs of energy criss-crossing from the stage to the seats as connections were made between those in spirit and those in the audience. Those arcs would have varied in thickness; some would be as thick as rope, others would be just a faint trace of light. Depending on how the evening progressed those lines would shift throughout the night, many would interject and combine, some would become fat and chunky and off-shoots would spark out from these like lightening connecting striking other people. It was an ever-changing network of connections.

I had been touring for five years and was beginning to gain a real understanding of how the process worked. I knew that everything was driven by this invisible energy and that somehow patterns formed during each show. I would give a message to someone in the audience and by doing that I would create an energy connection to them. This would draw in other messages. Spirits were attracted to areas of the audience where connections had already been made. That night proved to be a prime example of this process.

It started with a very specific message which made a strong energy connection. I learned that the more accurate the message, the stronger the connection would be.

There was a man standing next to me. He was in spirit and he had appeared faintly in my mind earlier in the day. He was speaking to me in my mind and his words were clear and concise. He told me his name was Andy and he gave me the names of three women; Debbie, Carole and Angela. He was 55 and he spoke with a Scottish accent. He was looking over to a section of the audience on the left-hand side of the auditorium.

I walked across the stage so I was standing in line with where he was looking. He followed.

'I have a lovely man here called Andy. He's been with me for a few hours. He is in spirit. I get the number 55 and the names Debbie, Carole and Angela,' I said, addressing the area Andy was looking at.

Sometimes the messages come through jumbled, the details and names are hard to make out but this was crystal clear and as soon as I said the names I heard a gasp from the audience and saw a hand go up. I could feel the connection being made between Andy in spirit and the woman in the audience. It was instant. It felt like a surge of electricity going through me. At that moment, if I had been looking through those imaginary psychic specs I believe I would have seen a bolt of blue light shoot out of Andrew, pass through me and arc across the audience to hit the person who was taking the message; the receiver.

She stood and explained that her name was Carole, she was with one of her sisters, Debbie, and had another sister, Angela. Her father, Andy, had died three years before and would have been 55 two weeks ago. I smiled.

'This message is definitely for you,' I told her

nodding my head. The confidence did not just come because the information was so specific. I knew and trusted it because I could feel the energy link between the gentleman in spirit and the woman. Her sister rose to stand next to her and I felt another surge.

I began the process of linking the living with their loved ones in spirit. Andy talked to them through me. He gave me information specific to his death and told me how his daughters were around his bedside when he passed.

'He thanks you for that,' I told the women. 'You made it much easier for him.'

He gave me another piece of information, this time less clearly, as if there was some interference.

'Was he something to do with the fire service or did he get badly burned in an accident?' I asked.

They confirmed that he had been a fireman but that luckily he was never injured in the line of duty. But I could actually smell burning flesh. It was turning my stomach.

'Are you sure? Was anyone else in your family burned in an accident?'

The women shook their heads.

Then I heard another name in my mind, again it sounded far off and quieter than the information Andy had given me. 'And who is, Mel or Melissa?'

They looked blankly at each other.

At that moment a woman three seats to the left of the sisters spoke out. I ushered her to stand. She did and as she stood another spirit appeared by the side of me. She was a woman and I could see she was badly burned down the left side of her face. Her skin was hanging in charred strips from her face and neck. I recoiled. I am human after all and no matter how many times I witness injuries they still make me jump. I steadied myself and told myself that this poor woman was not there to scare me. She was just showing me details in order to validate who she was to the person she wanted to link with.

I could feel another spark of energy zap through me as this injured lady connected with the lady who had taken the message and who was explaining that she had an aunt called Melissa who had died as a result of a house fire. A theme was beginning to build around that specific area of the audience. Melissa was giving me details, Andy was giving me details. Sometimes the paths crossed. Melissa had come in because I was talking to a fireman. That was the link. She mentioned twins and her niece confirmed that she was a twin but that her twin brother had died in childbirth. I then saw Melissa holding a baby.

'Your brother is here,' I explained. 'Your aunt is looking after him.'

It was like a psychic This Is Your Life.

Two names popped into my head; Joe and Arthur. Instinctively I knew they were also twins. I also knew one of them was gay but had hidden his sexuality throughout his life because he lived in a family where homosexual relationships were frowned upon. I had no idea which one of the ladies in the audience this information would relate to. It seemed disjointed from the two messages I was working with but I had to trust what I was receiving and asked the ladies who Joe and Arthur were.

'They are twins and one of them has a secret,' I said tactfully.

Again the women looked on blankly. I was offered more information.

'Joe was married and had children but... how can I put this... he preferred male company.' The audience laughed at my attempts to be diplomatic.

Someone else in the same area of the audience raised her hand and explained that her grandfather had twin brothers named Joseph and Arthur and that there had always been suspicion in the family that Joseph was gay. It was amazing and it was a process that I had seen replicated repeatedly over the years. It started with a single connection in a specific area of the audience and then widened out to bring in more and more links.

To begin with, when I started touring, these links had appeared irregularly and haphazardly. But increasingly over the years they had become more pronounced and five years in to my touring career they were becoming the norm. It was a pattern that I was fascinated to learn more about and I started to think long and hard about how and why it happens. I came up with a name for the process. I call it *message building*.

It starts with a clear hit. I've always had a problem with some of the hocus-pocus-type language some mediums use to dress up their work so I try and keep my descriptions simple and let the acts speak for themselves. The word 'hit' is a nice simple way to describe the act of a very specific message being taken by a receiver. When I ask a member of the audience 'who in your family lost the third finger on their left hand' and they answer incredulously 'that was my grandfather', that is a hit. It is a piece of information I am given by spirit that is so targeted and appears so random to anyone else that it can only be meant for the receiver. It is what spirits use to validate themselves to the people they are linking to.

A hit is the type of in-depth message that people are blown away by. I believe hits make connections between the spirit and the receiver so strong that they anchor the spirit to the world of the living and send out a signal into the afterlife that there is a powerful link that others can use. In life it is human nature to want to communicate with each other and to share ourselves as we are sociable creatures and the same is true in death. Think of it like a bar or a restaurant. The ones that attract the most custom are the ones that have customers in them. Most of us would walk past an empty restaurant because we'd feel the place would have no atmosphere. When we see somewhere with a lively feel to it we are drawn in.

Spirits want to connect with their loved ones and

if there is an opportunity to do that they will take it. So when they realise there is a pathway they are drawn to it. During shows that pathway is me. They listen in to the messages I am giving and, if there is a link or hook they recognise such as a subject they were familiar with in life, they come through too. It helps to think of each message as a fishing line that stretches out from me and each piece of information as a baited hook. Others in spirit tend to be drawn to these hooks if they can associate with them and when they do they take the bait. The whole system is orchestrated because unbelievably, there are always clusters of people who have things in common sitting near to each other in the audience. As the links between the spirits and their loved ones increase, so more are attracted to the area in which the links are being made. It can end up getting pretty crowded on stage when the message building process is in full swing!

It is an incredible phenomenon and one I was desperate to learn more about. My level of understanding began to grow deeper and deeper. I started looking at what I was doing differently. I took a more objective approach which at first seemed bizarre as I had always been someone who had bags of empathy and had always become emotionally involved in my work. I still maintained that emotional link with the audience and the people I was reading for but after the shows I started to make notes about what had happened and thought about theories to explain the unexplainable.

I started to see the patterns and the links between messages. I tried to look at things in a scientific, analytical way. I wondered why the process of message building was happening. What was causing it? Cynics might put these links down to coincidence but there was nothing coincidental about them. They were happening every night and the links between the messages were becoming more discernible.

Nothing like it had happened back in the days when I was reading for single people or small groups of two or three. Even when I first started doing demonstrations in halls there were never any patterns that were so obvious. The key had to be the number of people in the room and the number of connections I was making. Something was causing them and something was also allowing me to handle them and juggle them with increasing expertise. To begin with, as my audiences grew, I struggled to filter the information but the more the crowds grew and the more the connections between the living and the dead were made, the more adept I became at controlling what was happening. It was as if I had a psychic muscle which I had been exercising all my life and which, suddenly, was getting the benefit of steroid injections.

When I really thought about what I was doing I realised that I no longer just heard a message as a thought pattern in my head, I felt it through my mind and body. The anticipation before the shows was palpable. There was an atmosphere that I could feel. At some point in our lives we have all walked into a room and felt an atmosphere. We talk about houses being homely or assign bad feelings to them and I think that atmosphere we feel is created by an energy that permeates through every living thing and beyond into the afterlife. That energy was what allowed me to speak to spirit. I had become so attuned to it that it flooded through me. The energy was the key to everything. It is not just the medium by which messages are conveyed, like radio waves, it is the message itself. It is the essence of us all. It was a build up of this energy which created the atmosphere I felt every night. It was made from a combination of the love and emotions of those on Earth plane and those in spirit. It was the fundamental force that drove everything and when hundreds of living people entered a theatre, each with the hope, belief and anticipation of connecting with someone in spirit that energy became a tornado.

Life force: the energy at the centre of everything

According to science, the world we know is made of matter and that matter behaves the way it does because of rules imposed on it. Light behaves the way it does because it follows the laws of physics; water behaves the way it does because of the laws of chemistry. Scientific rules govern everything; me, you, the houses we live in, the cars we drive, the planes we fly in, the phones we talk into and the televisions we watch. This idea is what clever people call materialism and according to materialism there is no other realm apart from the one we live in; no spirit world, no afterlife, no heaven or hell. While I am fascinated with science and believe it will answer all our questions in time I don't agree completely with the theory that there is nothing other than this world and life because of events that I witnessed many years ago which changed my life forever.

I was a young nurse working in the South London Hospital for Women and I witnessed the exact moment one of the patients passed away. Because I saw that moment through the eyes of a medium the scene I witnessed was earth-shattering. I believe no one else was supposed to see that event other than me. It was my validation. Something somewhere was showing it to me to tell me to trust in my ability. It is a story I have told many times before but only in the last years have I begun to understand the mechanics of what happened.

My shift had taken me to the oncology ward. It was the last place terminal patients were sent. It was where women in the advanced stages of cancer were taken to die. It was a large, airy room lined on either side with beds which were enclosed by linen curtains. On the whole the ward was silent, every now and then a cough, a painful sigh or a groan would break the still air. The people in there were extremely ill. Most were sedated. As I walked down the ward at the start of my shift I passed a bed with the curtain drawn around it. I could hear the faint breaths of the patient inside behind the linen and I knew that she was not long for this world. From my medical experience I could hear it in the gentle rattle in her throat and chest. She was in the advance stages of lung cancer.

Her name was Anne and she had been administered her final dose of medicine; the strong morphine based mixture they gave terminally ill patients in those days to ease their last hours. Along with one of the other nurses on duty with me I pulled back the curtain to check on the patient. She was frail and lifeless. Her skin was sallow and stretched across her drawn face like tracing paper, it was pale and transparent. She was in a deep sleep and appeared peaceful.

I looked around the cubicle and saw a man sitting

in the chair by the side of her bed. He was looking at her intently and his hands were resting on his lap. I knew he was in spirit and instinctively I knew he was her husband. He was waiting for her. He had come to meet his wife and to help guide her into the afterlife. He seemed totally unaware of my presence and the fact that I could see him.

I leant over and whispered quietly in her ear.

'It's ok to let go now love. Your husband is here for you. He's come to take you.' I gently stroked her cheek and as I did her eyes fluttered ever so slightly and then she was gone.

What happened next was hard to describe. The air above Anne seemed to open up. It started from a tiny pinprick. It was similar to the effect you see on a television screen when there is a dead pixel. There was single point above her chest that was a different light intensity to everything around it. It grew slowly bigger and as it did I could feel it; it filled the room with an amazing sense of peace and love. Then something rose from Anne, it was like a ball of bright white gas that drifted from her and as it did I felt a very slight breeze. Although I had never witnessed anything like that before I realised that I was watching Anne's soul leave her body. And as it did the spirit of the man sitting with her changed form. The vision I had seen dissolved into the same form that had risen from Anne; a ball of what appeared to be glowing gas. This rose to join with the substance that had emerged from Anne and together they became one and drifted slowly into the air and up to the glowing light. After just seconds they all became one and as slowly as the process started the light shrunk down and down, never losing its brightness until it became just a tiny pinprick of brilliance in the air again. And then, as suddenly at it appeared, it vanished. All that was left was me, my colleague who had witnessed none of this and the body of Anne, still and at peace.

I knew then that I had been privileged to witness something so profound and beautiful that I would never see it again. I was being shown how spirit worked.

I think about the events of that day often and increasingly I have wondered what exactly it was that left Anne's body. We call it a soul because that's what religions call it but what was it made of and what was its purpose? The soul is seen as something ephemeral and intangible but I had the belief that it must be made of something. Just because we cannot see something with our human eyes does not mean it doesn't exist.

As circumstances led me to think harder about my work and the process involved I wanted to know more about what had happened there; were there any rules governing the process, where had the soul gone?

Philosophers, religious leaders and even scientists have attempted to work out what a soul is for thousands of years. In many traditions it is seen as the immortal essence of a person and is without form. In 1907 a doctor in the US named Duncan

MacDougall even went as far as trying to weigh a soul. He proposed that the human soul weighed 21 grams. In an experiment he placed six dying patients on beds fitted with sensitive weighing mechanisms and measured them just before and just after they died. In each case he recorded a sudden, unexplained weight loss of 21 grams which he said was not caused by any natural process. He concluded that the sudden loss could only be explained by the soul leaving the body and that the soul must therefore weigh 21 grams. He repeated the experiment on dogs but recorded no weight loss at the time of death and so surmised that dogs do not have souls. I know for a fact this is wrong because I regularly get dogs and all other sorts of other animals coming through to me when I do readings. MacDougall's notes were published in an academic journal but his findings and methods have long been questioned by other academics.

I decided to leave the question of whether or not a soul weighs anything to the boffins. Personally I'm not sure it shares the same qualities or follows the same rules as matter does on earth.

It is my belief that a soul, or spirit, is made from a form of energy – a bit like electricity. I came to this conclusion because of the way the process works when I am on stage. Messages build in intensity and are attracted to other messages as though there is some form of magnetism drawing them together in clumps. I believe that this energy is life essence and is one of the fundamental ingredients of the universe, not just the universe we inhabit but the universe of the afterlife as well. It is the one constant force that bridges across the realm of the living and the realm of the dead and which makes us what we are.

In each of us there is a ball of this energy. Maybe one day we will be able to put it under a microscope and study it but I'm not sure we will ever be allowed to replicate it because it is so powerful and dangerous – anyone with the ability to harness it will have power over life and death. It is the stuff of science fiction. People may say I am mad for thinking this but if you told a person 200 years ago that one day we would all be carrying shiny squares around in our pockets that you can touch and get instant information from all over the world from you would have been locked up! Somewhere bound up in the laws of quantum physics or relativity there will be answers.

So how does the energy work? Since I started touring I have learned how to harness it and make it work in an environment where there are lots of people and lots of messages all coming through at the same time. I've learned that there is a skill to making my gift work in larger audiences. I try to tell the audience what is happening as the evening progresses and provide a commentary which I hope is helpful. Psychic energy can travel across time and space and connect people. Once you trust in it and let it in by accepting the truth that it is from spirit world, it will become part of you. It connects to something inside your body. In my case that connection can be so strong that I take on aspects of the personality of the spirit that the energy is from; their gait, their vocabulary, how they felt at the ends of their lives. It is quite incredible and fascinating. For people who are not mediums, that connection can feel comforting and loving.

Just like electricity in a wall socket we can't see this energy but if you took the cover off the socket and put your finger in it you'd feel it. When we die the plate comes off the switch. The body that houses it dies and the energy has no reason to stay in its vessel anymore. The ball of energy will be released and it passes over into the afterlife, which is its natural habitat. I think of the afterlife as another dimension; a place within the universe that exists in parallel with our world. It is where energy resides and was there from the beginning of time. Little bits of energy break off from this world and come to inhabit us and give us our souls. Psychic energy is neither created nor destroyed, the same as all energy. It just changes form. It passes through the universe, between the worlds of the living and the dead. Sometimes it is recycled, which leads to the question of reincarnation, a subject I'm still getting to grips with. I definitely think souls come back in other bodies. The miracle of life only happens because energy enters the cell that is fertilised and sometimes that energy has the imprint of the person that it previously belonged to. We talk about people being old souls. These are people, usually young children, who have energy within them that has been passed on. For example my daughter, Fern, has always been an old soul. She was street wise and acted beyond her years from a very early age. She is four years younger than my daughter Rebecca yet she is several lifetimes ahead of her in terms of being worldly wise and that's because when I conceived her, in addition to the genes John and I passed to her, she was also created with energy that gave her a soul and that energy had been recycled from other people, maybe thousands over time.

There are two elements that must be in alignment for the energy connection between the living and the dead to take place. Firstly there is the spiritual element. There needs to be trust and love. These two factors are what fuel the process. Without trust in spirit there can be no openness. If you do not trust in spirit and in what it shows you there will be no connection. The easiest way I can explain this is by looking at what happens during my shows. There is an unwritten bond of trust between me, the audience and spirit. Without that trust it simply would not work. As the messages come through I have to trust that they are from spirit and that they are meant for people in the audience. When people in the audience hear a message that they believe is for them, they have to trust that it is and take that message. Once that trusting bond is established, the magic can happen.

Love is what draws spirit to us and it is what we

send out to attract it. It is another form of bond that links us to the people we know who have passed over. I think it is largely what psychic energy is made from. As we grow and develop through life, our energy, which sits in the centre of us, changes and develops with us. The more love we have in our lives, the more our energy is nourished and the more love shown to us on earth plane, the more we are drawn back here after we die to link with our loved ones.

That is the spiritual side. But there is also a physical part to the equation which allows me and other mediums to do what we do. I believe that inside all of our brains there is a structure, maybe like a switch or a valve or even a chemical that works to unlock the part of our minds which open to spirit and allow the energy in us to connect with the energy around us. We all have this structure, it's a part of the human body just like a heart or a lung but over time it has been used less and less so it becomes weak. Modern life doesn't allow us to use this function as much as we would have done thousands of years ago. Today we have distractions in the form of computers and televisions and mobile phones, we rarely have the opportunity to listen to our bodies and minds and to follow our natural intuitiveness which is what this structure in our brains facilitates. All this interference affects both our spiritual lives and our brains and takes us further away from the wonders of spirit. We can reclaim our spiritual heritage however. I have noticed that the more I am exposed to high levels of psychic energy through the experience of theatre shows, the more developed my ability to connect with spirit seems to get. It's like I am exercising a muscle. We all have the same muscles in our arms, some people work them to get them toned or big and bulky, others don't and get bingo wings. Our arms all look completely different yet we all have the same underlying physiology in there.

All this theory – that we have a natural ability to connect with an energy that resides in another dimension and that is the essence of our souls – goes against all scientific understanding. In science the belief is that your brain's role is to send messages to every part of your body and to control what you do and how you think, which is true, but I believe the brain is capable of much more than that. For the very few, the psychic process happens in an innate way. I am lucky enough to be able to conduct it naturally as I have never been aware of trying to link to spirit consciously. I wouldn't even know where to start. It is something that just happens in my head.

Our understanding of the brain is still so basic. Scientists who study it say we are hundreds of years away from knowing what is really going in our minds. We have only just scratched the surface and there are so many more wonders to uncover. For example scientists have only recently learned how the brain develops by building pathways between certain cells. As we grow the brain changes every day. Every new experience we have creates new connections between brain cells. This is how we learn and remember things. Because of this process, the brain can rewire itself and compensate for functions lost through injuries, which explains why people who lose their sight report increased sensitivity in other senses such as hearing. I think this process also allows people who exercise their psychic side to grow a more spiritual brain.

I hope that one day science will be able to explain what happens to me when I connect with spirit. My belief is that physics must have a lot to do with my work because it is concerned with the study of energy and forces. Throughout history science has provided the answer to many phenomena that were first thought of as supernatural. Science told us that the Earth was round, that planets moved through space and that the stars were distant suns. It explained how our planet was formed and it explained why apples fall to the ground from trees instead of floating into the sky. There is still so much to discover and it would surprise the sceptics to know that I put my faith in science to provide the answers.

There are a few brave academics who are already testing what the scientific community describes as the paranormal. Usually their work gets drowned out by the sceptic community. One such scientist is a man named Rupert Sheldrake. He is an author and former biochemist and plant physiologist. He studied at Cambridge and was awarded a Royal

Society Fellowship, which in short means he is a clever bloke.

He is one of the few researchers to approach the unexplained with an open mind. Throughout his career he studied phenomena such as telepathy and psychokenisis (the ability to influence objects with the mind). Because of this, his work has been criticised by sceptics who feel it is not scientifically valid. After becoming disillusioned with what he believed was the stifling nature of modern science, he went on a year and half spiritual retreat in India where he wrote his first book, *A New Science of Life*. In it he came up with a theory about how some living creatures appear to know how to perform certain tasks without learning them and appear to behave in unison in certain circumstances. For example how do spiders know how to spin intricate webs without learning from other spiders and how do flocks of starlings swarm together and behave as if they are one single entity? Rupert believed these puzzles could be explained by some undiscovered field or force that carried information that all living things could tap into. He called this idea 'morphic resonance'. The implication of the theory was that memory is inherent in nature and that the mind could function outside the body. Certain paranormal events could be explained because ideas in one person's mind could be shared and shaped by a link with another mind through this force. I find this idea fascinating but while the book gained some positive reviews, others thought it was a crazy idea. One high-brow journal asked if it was a book which should be burned.

The academic community began to turn on him but this did not put him off and he continued to develop his ideas. He started looking at telepathy and conducted numerous studies into one of the common unexplained physical sensations we have all had at some time in our lives where we feel we are being stared at. He discovered that in 55 per cent of cases, people could correctly tell through intuition that they were being stared at. His conclusion was that we all have a heightened perceptive ability but rarely realise it or act upon it.

In one famous experiment Rupert tried to prove whether dogs are telepathic. He studied one specific hound, a psychic terrier called Jaytee who seemed to know instinctively when his owner was coming home, even when she arrived home unexpectedly. Rupert carried out over 100 tests to see how many times Jaytee's intuition was correct. Amazingly the dog knew that his owner was on the way home 55 per cent of the time.

Despite the rigours of his studies Rupert was again ridiculed by certain sections of the scientific community for approaching a subject that many labelled pseudoscience and dogmatically viewed as impossible.

Personally I think it is very sad that someone who sticks their head above the parapet and tackles subjects that millions of people are interested in and give credence too can be viewed with such derision. No matter how 'unscientific' mediumship and telepathy appear, they cannot be dismissed because they do happen. Every night I walk on stage and very strange things happen. The processes are repeated again and again. Messages build and are hooked in by other messages. Even before I get to the venues I perform at, strange things are stirring. Information is popping into my head. Hours before a recent show in Australia I was travelling in the car on the way to the town where the show was being staged and suddenly I turned to John.

'I have someone here. She's a little girl, her name is Charlotte, she is 7,' I told him.

We had not been talking about anything specific. I was just listening to the radio minding my own business when she popped into my head. I could feel her and hear her say her name in her child's voice. It was so clear I jumped and, because we were a long way off the show and I had not been thinking about anything in particular, it unsettled me a bit (you'd think I would be used to it by now but sometimes I get the jitters too, especially where children in spirit are concerned).

I could feel her there for the rest of the day and when I got on stage hers was the first name I spoke. She was there with me in spirit waiting. Immediately a woman in the front row stood to tell me she had nursed a little girl called Charlotte in hospital. Charlotte gave me the name Jane. The woman nodded.

'Jane was Charlotte's mum,' she said.

Then I started to sense a little boy in spirit who was coming through with Charlotte. I could see him in my mind's eye, first appearing faintly and then becoming more defined, like a television tuning in. The name Christopher popped into my head and I sent it out into the audience.

'Who is Christopher?' I asked.

The woman who had stood to take Charlotte's message was with a friend. She stood up too. Her mouth was agape.

'Christopher was my son,' she explained in awe.

Episodes such as that happen to me all the time. They are too common and accurate to be coincidences. So what is happening if not some form of psychic event? Rupert's ideas about a universal field and my experience of psychic energy may not be exact answers but they go some way to explaining the remarkable experiences I have been lucky enough to engage in.

At present we are chipping away at the edges. We have genetics now and we are starting to understand what goes on inside the tiny cells in our body. We are gaining more and more knowledge but we are just on the fringes. Perhaps one day, when the mysteries have been unlocked, everyone will have a well-honed psychic ability. They may look at the work I did and laugh at how crude early mediums were. Perhaps connecting with our loved ones in spirit will be as simple as making a phone call. In this respect I am the equivalent of the first television set; a massive bulky thing with a black and white screen which needs to warm up before the picture comes through. In future we may receive messages in HD.

Just because we do not fully understand the incredible, does not mean we should dismiss it. On the contrary, we should investigate it and ask questions about it. As long as there is measured debate and a spirit of curiosity, rather than dogmatic refusal to entertain that there is something happening, then one day we will know the answers.

PART TWO

Questions of life and death

Why do people die?

To so many people death seems like the cruellest part of being human. It is something we all experience in life. Each of us will lose a loved one at some point in our lives and then each of us will die. Of everything we go through in life, death is the one inevitability, which can seem a bit grim at times because on the whole, most people do not want to die. There are three main reasons for this. Firstly, many see death as a painful process and something that is arrived at after illness, discomfort or an agonising accident. Secondly most of us enjoy life and have people in our lives who we love. We don't want to leave them and we don't want to stop doing the things we enjoy. And thirdly there is the fear of the unknown. It takes trust and faith to realise that there is an afterlife and unfortunately many people are persuaded against a belief that there is another life after death because of sceptical voices.

Thankfully, I have been privileged to shine a light on death for thousands of people during the hundreds of stage shows I have performed around the country and abroad and hopefully during these I have shown to many doubters that there is something else and that they needn't let the three fears of death cast a cloud over their lives.

We can't ignore the fact that some deaths, as experienced on earth plane, can be painful but that pain passes as soon as we pass. It is replaced by peace and bliss. There is no pain in the afterlife because pain is something which we experience through our bodies. When we die we discard our bodies and with them the ability to be hurt. We are set free from the ailments and disabilities that held us back when we lived. Over the years I have received messages from thousands of people in spirit who suffered during life and in every case there is no hint of pain in the afterlife, only relief and freedom.

There is also no sense of loss in the afterlife because our energy is always linked to our loved ones, living and dead. The love we have for each other when we are alive does not stop when we die. And as for fear of the unknown, well you only have to come to one of my shows to realise that the evidence of an afterlife is out there. All you have to do is look in the right place.

So why do we die? Well quite simply it is the natural order of things. Dying is part of the process of life, everything on the planet has a lifespan but unfortunately we are not bristlecone pine trees which can live for thousands of years. We are lucky if we live to 100. We have a short lifespan in relation to some organisms and a long one in relation to others. We live on a single planet with limited space and if no one died our part of the physical universe would soon become overcrowded. Life is finite, it has to be. It is the bit afterwards that is infinite! Death is part of the overall plan. Some tragic deaths appear to be unfairly random and against the natural chronological order of things, such as when children die. However, I believe we all die when we are meant to. The same applies to all forms of life. I love my garden at home and recently bought a pallet of border flowers from the garden centre. They were all from the same batch, they were all healthy and of the same age and size. They all cost the same and I took care to make sure they were all healthy when I chose them. They all got the same amount of attention when I planted them but for some unknown reason one died. There was no apparent reason why, it was simply its turn to go. While I was digging it up for the compost heap I realised that its demise was a good analogy for what happens to humans. We are a species, we are born and we die. Some survive longer than other but in our bodily form none of us survive forever.

We are emotional creatures and we love each other and when what we perceive as the natural order of things is upset, when someone dies out of sync, we get upset and angry. We talk of people dying too soon and we question why it happens. Losing children is the wrong way round after all isn't it? Parents should not out live offspring. But people die. That is the fact of the matter. They get sick and they die, sometimes they don't get sick and they die. And the reason for it is that the energy we hold inside us that makes us who we are is not meant to be held on to. It is part of the balance of the wider universe we have yet to fully understand.

Science and medicine have made huge strides in keeping people alive and beating diseases. Undoubtedly this is a good thing. However, I am not always sure that it's right to use science as a way of overcoming death, or at least holding it at bay when death is the natural progression. There are times when people should be allowed to go. It is in our nature to want to keep people alive. We all have a survival instinct and know how precious life is and should most definitely follow that and prevent suffering with medicine if we can. However, most people know when it is their time to go and would want to go with dignity. I would never want to lose my dignity and face years of suffering just so I could live for a few extra years or to reach a landmark, for example to be 100. I would rather die at 80 and enjoy life. Quality of life is the most important thing. Being involved in life and receiving and giving love is the thing that feeds our energy. That cannot happen for people who are in vegetative states on life support machines with no hope of recovery. Their energy is stuck. So while we have the ability to keep people alive when they have suffered catastrophic events, it is only their bodies being kept alive and not their personalities or their souls. I have faith in spirit world so I know that there is another life after this and I believe that we should trust in the deep spiritual instinct we have and release people when it is their time to go.

The question of what happens spiritually when science and death meet becomes even more interesting when you consider a widely-held prediction of how humans and machines will evolve in the coming decades. Ray Kurzweil is a renowned computer scientist and 'futurist' – he studies current trends and uses them to predict the future. He also advises Google so he's someone whose views are taken seriously. In his 2005 book called *The Singularity Is Near* he predicted that by the mid 2040s humans will have developed technology so advanced and intelligent it will allow us to overcome obstacles such as illness and even perhaps death itself. Man and machine will integrate in both the physical and virtual worlds at a point in history called the singularity. It is a radical idea that sounds like science fiction but one which received a lot of attention and serious consideration when the book was published. But if we no longer died, where would that leave us spiritually? How could the energy in us ever be released and reused? I believe that although the idea is interesting, while humans certainly have an inbuilt desire to prolong life, technology and science will only ever be allowed to delay the inevitable. Death will still be as inevitable as it always has been.

What happens when we die?

Once the body lets go of life, the beauty of the afterlife becomes apparent. A passing takes a split second and in that instant we are released from our bodies and any pain and suffering we may have experienced. Passing over is easier for some than it is for others. Death can be a confusing business, not just for the living as we learn to cope without loved ones. It can also be confusing for those who have passed. I have discovered that this can be the case when a spirit has unfinished business on Earth plane.

For example I was on stage at a show in the north of England when I felt an energy push through into my mind. As had happened in so many other cases the lady in spirit came through because there was a hook from a previous message. I had been giving a reading to a family who were involved in a feud and the lady in spirit, Sylvia, came through. She had passed just the previous week and since her passing she had been aware of infighting among her family. She wanted to get the message across to her loved ones to put aside their differences and stop bickering. Life is too short, she told me. I chuckled to myself at her words, she was making a joke.

As soon as I gave the audience her name and explained that she had died just a week ago, a lady in the middle of the theatre stood to take the message and confirmed the details about the family disagreement.

Usually, when I feel that connection the flow of information I am given from spirit is clear and constant. But the connection I had with Sylvia seemed disjointed. Her passing had been so sudden it had left her slightly confused. I could tell it was the first time she had made contact from spirit. She seemed apprehensive.

'I can speak, will you hear me?' she was repeating in my mind.

She was not apologising for going but she told the receiver she couldn't hold on any longer.

I had the sense that she was feeling her way through the process.

'She is fully here,' I told the audience, 'but she is hesitant. She doesn't know how quickly she can let me have information.'

I had never experienced a reading like it. It was as if Sylvia's energy was suspended. And then it dawned on me.

'Has she been buried yet?' I asked the woman who had taken the message.

'No, she is being buried next week,' she answered.

That was why she was so confused. Her passing was unexpected and her remains had not been laid to rest. She had no closure and she was in some confusion about letting go fully.

A death is as individual as a life and while Sylvia was slightly disorientated by hers and needed the formality of a funeral to let go fully, the majority of spirits embrace the afterlife.

On a biological level, when a person dies their heart stops, their breathing stops, their blood stops circulating and their brain ceases to function. Their body dies and when it does their soul – the energy that made up the essence of who they were – passes over into another realm where they live on. We live in a different way. The difference is the body; the form and matter that we need on Earth and which makes us humans is useless in spirit. Our bodies come from nothing and they go to nothing but the energy within them is eternal.

The act of dying itself is not scary at all. At the point in our lives where we stop breathing and our body shuts down we reach a peaceful place, even if the circumstances are not. Even if someone is murdered, as they die they find peace no matter what the external circumstances are. And even though many who pass are aware they are dying and are fearful, they have lucid moments near death when their loved ones come to reassure them. No one dies alone. Even if the person who dies does not know anyone directly in spirit – even if they have no known dead relatives or friends – he or she will still be linked to the afterlife through ancestors who have passed and that link will enable them to be guided into spirit world. It is like a chain that stretches back through time. Spirits linked to us come at the point of death because they are familiar to us. For us on Earth plane heaven is unknown and they come to reassure us. They have walked the path before so they come to guide us and they reassure those who are reluctant to let go. They are drawn to us, we don't call them. I believe this because I don't call the dead when I go on stage. They are just there. The audience creates the link by trusting in the power of spirit and ringing the doorbell to heaven.

The fact that there is always someone waiting for us in spirit was brought vividly to life for me at a recent show. Two male spirits came through and I knew instinctively that they shared a family connection. In my mind's eye I saw a scene. One of the men in spirit was lying in a hospital bed. He was surrounded by machines which were keeping him alive. The other man, who was older, was standing at the foot of the bed and a woman was seated by the side of the bed, she was leaning over the man who was lying down and she was sobbing. The younger man in spirit had the clearest energy and told me his name was Ben. He wanted to speak to a lady called Julie. I also sensed the name Colin.

'I have a Ben here,' I explained to the audience. 'He is giving me the name Julie.'

A lady stood to take the message and as she did I felt a surge of energy from spirit. Bingo! She told me her name was Julie and that her husband was in spirit and his name was Ben.

'And who is Colin?' I asked.

'He's my father-in-law,' she answered.

'He is in spirit,' I knew this was the case. It was a statement rather than a question. She nodded. I explained the hospital scene I was being given. I felt a build up of pressure inside my head. It was Ben showing me the details of his death. I relayed this to Julie.

'There was a terrible pressure inside his head,' I said.

Julie explained that Ben had died from a brain haemorrhage.

The reading was extremely emotional. Julie didn't have to say anything, she just nodded her head in recognition as I described how she had been there at the bedside while her husband lay dying and how, unbeknown to her at the time, Ben's father Colin had been there waiting to guide his son into the afterlife.

'They are together,' I told her. 'He didn't die alone. His dad came to get him.'

What is the afterlife?

The afterlife has puzzled mankind for hundreds of thousands of years. What is it, where is it, what does it look like? They are deep questions that no one really knows the answer too. Hollywood has tried. One of my favourite films is Ghost, mainly because I fancied Patrick Swayze and because of the scene where Whoopi Goldberg, who plays a medium, has spirits lining up to use her to contact their relatives. It always makes me laugh and it's not a million miles away from the truth.

Different cultures have different ideas and representations. The concept of an afterlife as represented in religion is a way for us to visualise a space where our souls can rest and inhabit. Christian religions believe in a heaven and a hell which have certain earthly characteristics. In the traditional view, Heaven is the sky and has white clouds, angels with harps and golden gates. The sky was probably chosen because at the time, human knowledge of what was above us and out in space was even more limited than it is today and the sky and stars were mysterious. Hell was below us. Again, because geology was in its infancy no one really knew about the Earth's core and tectonic plates. Instead they believed under our feet lay another realm full of demons, fire and brimstone. I don't think either of these ideas translates into the true nature of the afterlife for the simple reason that it is not anchored in the physical realm and so does not have the characteristics we are familiar with. It does not use space and time as we do and so it is not something you can touch, see, hear or taste with your normal senses. It doesn't fill space like our world does because spirits are not made of the same stuff we are. They don't live in houses, they don't eat or wear clothes and they don't move in the way we perceive movement. They don't take up any room yet they are everywhere and all around us. Their world over lays ours, like those children's books where several layers of printed plastic sit on top of each other to create a complete picture. Spirit world exists in conjunction with our world and is made of energy which stretches into our world like an invisible umbilical cord. This I believe because it is there every night I stand on stage and give readings. Spirits are with me, and with all of us, at every step we take through life. They do not reside in a far off mystical realm.

All this stuff is hard to get your head around. Believe me, I know! I've been trying to work it out for years. In order to try and comprehend what the afterlife is you have to change the way you look at things. You could question the whole concept.

'If every person and thing that ever lived goes to this place, how can they all fit Sally?' you could ask.

The doubt exists because you are looking at it

from the viewpoint of what you know, and that is that physical people inhabit physical space. When we die we are no longer physical. The solid form, our vehicles – our bodies – stay here. What leaves is our energy, which doesn't have mass or matter.

Another way to look at it is that we live in a realm that is a layer of a whole, like an onion. There are layers around us that we are not aware of. But that are all connected. And that means we can call up those within the afterlife layers with just a thought. For example my lovely granddad, who is in spirit, is with me all the time. I carry a link to his energy in my heart and I know at times when I need him I can think of him and he will be right next to me. His energy is a thought away as is the energy of all spirits.

It is my belief that the key to understanding what the afterlife and the energy that lies at the heart of it really is lies in the realm of science, possibly an area such as quantum mechanics. There are all kinds of mysteries and mind-boggling puzzles that great minds are trying to unravel at the edges of human understanding. Under the border between France and Switzerland near Geneva there is the huge Large Hadron Collider which is investigating the tiniest fragments of matter to see what lies inside them. Scientists there are hunting for something called the God Particle. Who knows what else they may discover, what other mysteries there are to be unveiled. Science, conducted with an open, inquisitive mind has the power to answer so much. I sometimes feel sorry for sceptics, because they spend all their time denying and don't embrace possibility. Anything seemingly miraculous, groundbreaking and pioneering will always be shouted down by people with a blinkered view of the possibilities of life. It wasn't so long ago in historical terms that people who said the Earth orbits the Sun were called heretics.

While our souls do not have physical form in the afterlife they do have memory because when they come through they recall events, people, places and feelings. They remember things and give me information so that people in the audience can connect and get validation. They recall happy situations to make the receiver feel happy. They will recognise and remember the memory and share it with the receiver because, on the whole spirit, wants to please and want their loved ones and relatives to be happy and to be secure in the knowledge that they are at peace. For this reason sometimes they show themselves in situations where their loved ones will feel comforted.

Sometimes the information is less pleasant. Sometimes they want justice for a wrong that was done to them in life. They are not vengeful but they have a deep sense of fairness. Quite often they use details and information about their deaths as a way to connect to their loved ones as each death is individual and often very private. This can be unpleasant for me as sometimes I feel how they felt when they passed. At one show in the Home

Counties I stood on stage choking and spluttering as I underwent the sensation of having fluid pouring down the back of my nose and throat. It wasn't water. It was blood. I could taste the warm metallic liquid. I was cold and shivering. But around me I could sense a warm glow, pulling me towards it. It wasn't in one specific place. It seemed to be pulling me from all angles at the same time and I felt an uncontrollable urge to let myself go and be pulled towards it and towards the warmth. It was afterlife. I was being pulled into the afterlife. And then I felt safe. It was an intense and unsettling experience. The spirit I was connected to was replaying its earthly death using me as a projection screen. I have found that the more my gift has developed, the more I feel what spirits felt at the end of their lives. It is one of the drawbacks of having such a finely tuned psychic antenna.

That traumatic reading culminated with the spirit telling its loved ones: 'I am safe where I am.' She came through to explain the peace of the afterlife and that despite the traumatic scenes when she passed, it did not matter because she was in a beautiful place.

They also show us their own personal heaven as we would perceive it in Earth plane. For example at a show on the south coast the spirit of a young girl came to me. She was looking for her mother in the audience and gave me her name and her mother's name and the number of the house she lived in.

Her mother took the message. The girl had been an animal lover when she was alive and as I connected with her my head was filled with an image of her in a sunny field surrounded by cute animals. She was laughing and rolling in the long grass with puppies and kittens. This was the afterlife she wanted her mother to know she was in. It was her representation of heaven and she was showing it to her mother to give her comfort. It was extremely touching.

While the afterlife is a beautiful place for all those that pass, what we do here on Earth does have implications for how we are received on the other side. The people who have gone before us ensure that they look after us and in the same way, if we do dreadful things here, I think when we go to spirit those same people ensure that somehow we are punished. I don't know how. It is one of the big questions I am trying to work out. I have a theory around the idea of reincarnation. Perhaps we come back here to Earth to make amends and cleanse our energy until it is pure enough to pass into the afterlife. That's not to say that every new born baby was a potential murderer in another life! But I feel the idea holds water; you don't get to the good place until you have made good. None of us are born with halos over our heads. Human beings make mistakes and have emotions and choices and decisions to make that are not always pleasant. That is part of life today.

How we conduct ourselves and how we love

each other also has a lot to do with what happens when we pass because love fuels our energy. If you give it out in life you get it back in the afterlife, even though it can be painful to love because we lose loved ones. I always say that the price for loving someone is grief but in the afterlife it is a price worth paying because grief stays put on Earth when we die. Instead we take the love with us. In life we build it up, it's like a savings account. The more love you put in your energy bank, the better the return when you die and cash it in. Every night I say on stage that messages can only come through because of love. When I talk about love I do not just mean the passionate kind. Love is all encompassing. You can love your kids, your animals, you can love life and you can love yourself (but be careful of vanity and selfishness).

Is my life mapped out for me?

The energy was skipping between spirits. All the messages were related to each other in some way. There was a network of psychic energy stretching across the venue. I had just finished a reading which related to a boy who was suffering from cancer when I got the name Daniel and a warm feeling in the middle of my head. The number 19 popped into my head. There was also a link to New Zealand.

The woman who took the message explained that Daniel was her grandson. He had died on October 19th of a stroke and had family in New Zealand.

She was sobbing as she talked to him through me.

It seemed so unfair. Daniel had been just 15 when he passed.

I tried to comfort her.

'He had to go,' I calmed. 'He couldn't have lived. There was something wrong in his head.'

It seemed so cruel but Daniel was at peace and he was still with his family, keeping close and connected to them through the love they had for him.

One of the hardest things for people to accept is the death of a child. It upsets the natural order of things but everyone goes when it is their time, no matter how sad that might be for those of us left behind. So many children come through to me at shows it can be overwhelming. I have to keep reminding myself of this one constant; that our lives are mapped out and that what happens to us and the ones we love happens for reasons we don't understand.

At another show a child came through. I saw her death. She had been on a horse. She fell off and broke her neck. She died there on the ground. It was an event that happened many years in the past but a lady who knew her and who had a horse in the stables where the accident happened took the message.

'Her soul is where your horse is kept, it could be spooked in the month of October because that's when she died and that's when her energy is strongest,' I explained.

The lady nodded. Her horse did indeed behave erratically every October. The little girl was coming through to let everyone know she was safe and she was where she was supposed to be.

When several children come through together on the same evening it becomes emotionally draining. And although I try to remember that they are happy and at peace where they are, I still find it heart-wrenching to communicate with them because, as a mother and grandmother myself, I can understand how painful it must be for the parents who lose children. At one memorable show in

Somerset several children came in, one after the other. They had all grown up and died in the local area. My head was spinning.

Initially a lady teacher who worked at one of the local schools came through from spirit and bought with her a young boy. When their message had been taken a little girl came through, followed by another little boy. The teacher was taking care of them as they presented themselves. The children were drawn to the energy of each other as the message built. It was an incredible thing to witness. Children are born untainted and open to spirit. We taint them as they grow by telling them there is no such thing as ghosts and that spirits do not exist. We do it out of a false sense of protection because we do not want them to be scared of the unexplained. When a child dies their energy is still pure.

Every message from a child in spirit is still like the first, even at this stage of my life after all the years I have been giving them, and that particular message was very special and memorable.

I believe in fate and destiny. Our biological clocks are predetermined largely by the genes we inherit from our parents. Even the lifestyle choices we make that influence when we die are affected by our genetic make-up. Our characteristics and personalities are mapped out because they come from the body we inhabit. The time and date we die isn't determined by the soul, it is determined by the body and I think that is pretty much set. When it's your time to go, it is your time to go, whether that seems unfair or not. You can influence it some degree, like the brave women who elect to have mastectomies to stop them getting cancer when they learn they carry a specific gene. They have reset their death clock. Ultimately however, I don't think we can cheat death, it gets us when it is meant to.

I also think what happens in life is mapped out for us. Life is full is coincidences that suggest there is a plan and that we are following a blueprint that has been designed for us. Take identical twins for example. There are many stories of identical twins being separated at birth and going off to live with different families without contact. But when they are reunited in later life it transpires that their lives have followed very similar paths. They've married people with the same name, done similar jobs, they have the same taste in music and clothes and have had similar life experiences. It is almost as if they have both been following a predetermined path. As if their lives were mapped out for them before they were born. Maybe something is written into our atoms, like a plan but on a deeper level than DNA, something that doesn't just determine physical characteristics but predetermines behaviour and situations and the choices we make.

I am not a believer in luck. I think we are either negative or positive and there is no doubt in my mind that once again, using the energy explanation, negative attracts negative and positive attracts positive. In life we have negative experiences, many of which can't be avoided. We will all suffer at one time or another. What determines how that affects you is how you deal with it. If you are the type of person who meets negative with negative, you will attract negativity. We all know people who bring the atmosphere of a room down and who seem to suck the joy from a situation. These people have chosen to side with negativity. Their energy is negatively charged. My glass is always half full. It is a hard mindset to maintain sometimes. I have been through tough situations but I have looked at my work and tried to take positives from it. Sometimes you have to meet misfortune and accept that it was meant to be and if you cannot do anything to change it, move forward positively in the best way you can.

While the future is set for us, we do not always have to go into it blindly. There are ways we can see what the future has in store for us. For example, I've always fancied learning more about astrology. I have met some really good astrologers who have known my life just from my date and time of birth. It is an uncanny skill. I also think that when you look at seers and astrologists going back through history, they knew stuff. Every civilisation has had soothsayers, oracles and mystics. Who am I to doubt them? I look at my stars and often they are bang on. And probably the most powerful tool we have at our disposal is our own intuition. Those hunches and feelings we all get are signs from beyond the realm of our senses. Use them and take notice of them because believe me, they are being given to you for a reason.

What is karma?

In religious terms the idea of karma has been around for thousands of years and stems from ancient Eastern religions such as Hinduism and Buddhism. In these belief systems karma is about actions, deeds and cause and effect.

More recently in the West, karma has been interpreted as being about payback and is often associated with sayings such as "what goes around comes around" and "you reap what you sow". In spiritualism some people see karma as a condition of spirit. Some believe controversially that karma carries over from one life to the next – so a person born with disabilities did something wrong in a previous life. I don't for a minute believe that disabled people are being punished and find the suggestion ridiculous.

I believe karma affects our energy and is a mechanism that keeps it balanced. In order for there to be a perfectly pure energy, there needs to be a balance between the negative and the positive. I think the karma balance happens over a life span, not many life spans. So if you throw a load of mud at someone or something, you will get it all back in some other way later in your life. If you hurt someone physically or mentally you will get hurt somewhere else down the road. Karma will ensure you get even. Karma can be a slap on the wrist and it can be orchestrated through spirits as they can tend to be moral arbiters who have a keen sense of justice. They like to set the balance straight.

This was demonstrated at one show where the spirit of a young child appeared to me on stage. He was a little boy. I got his name and straight away a woman's hand went up. Just after, a younger woman's hand went up too.

Out of fairness I told the stage manager to go to the first lady first.

'What made you put your hand up?' I asked. I couldn't feel a link between the spirit and the woman.

'I knew a boy by that name,' she said vaguely. Call me psychic but I knew she was lying.

The theatre suddenly felt tense. Her actions were making spirit unhappy. The audience felt it and went deadly quiet.

'Is the little boy for you?' I asked.

'Ok, no, it's not,' she admitted.

Message stealing is a big no-no in my view.

'So why did you put your hand up?'

She shrugged.

'Well we all want a message don't we? That's why we're here.'

I wish I could give everyone in the audience a message every night but I am constrained by my physical body and I simply can't. There is not enough time and I only have one mouth (which John would say is a blessing).

I tried to be understanding but the woman's selfish action and attitude annoyed me.

'This is a child in spirit who has come in and I respect children so much. He wants his mummy and you are not his mummy,' I admonished.

Then the lady got her karma thanks to spirit. Suddenly I knew she was there because she wanted a message from her mum. I told her and she nodded, eagerly anticipating that her mother would come through.

But a man came through instead. His name was Ken.

'Who is Ken?' I asked.

'I dunno,' she said, but I could tell she knew what I was talking about.

'He is your neighbour isn't he?'

She was giggling nervously and admitted that I was correct. She was getting defensive.

Then I saw an image of her with Ken's young nephew. She was being purposely mean to him.

'What did you do to his nephew?' I demanded.

Suddenly she shouted.

'He deserved it! He deserved everything he got.'

The whole audience gasped in unison.

'I don't think he did deserve it, did he?' I said menacingly. I'm not a naturally confrontational person but I was being given strength by spirit. They were using me to teach her a lesson. I walked over to the side of the stage she was on because I wanted the whole audience to see who she was.

'Your neighbour Ken, who is in spirit, wants you

to know that you have to go to spirit one day,' I told her. The implication hung in the air and with that she sat down. There was not a sound in the auditorium.

I tried to explain to the audience what had just happened.

'That was a very good example of be careful what you wish for. That lady stole a message from this little boy's mum. But spirit will slap your wrist. She wasn't very nice at all to Ken's nephew but she will have to face the consequences of that.'

How do spirits communicate with us?

This is one of the biggies! What mysterious process takes place that allows dead people to contact living people? As I've mentioned before, we are still a long way off understanding the mechanics of it – the nuts and bolts. What I do know is that at the heart of it is the psychic energy we all have inside us and which leaves our bodies when we die.

And although I can't draw you a diagram or write an equation that explains it, I do know from experience that there are different methods spirits use to make their presence felt on Earth plane. For people who do not have a medium's finely honed intuition, the main way spirit will communicate is with what I refer to as "signs". These can come in many forms. They can be visual and vivid, such as apparitions or what we call ghosts, or they can be more subtle and manifest themselves as thoughts and feelings.

It is quite rare to get a sign and you need to know what to look for. All the right elements have to be lined up for an individual to receive a sign. Much depends on the energy of the individual on that particular day and in that particular moment. It depends in that split second what you will see, hear, feel and experience. You have to be in synch

and open to the possibilities around you as sometimes spirit wants to come through but you are not
tuned in to its particular wavelength, or you might
only get an outline of them or a sense of them or
just a gut feeling. You need to trust that the nag-
ging feeling that there is someone there watching
you is real and that there is someone there.

So how do you know what a psychic sign is? Well
it may be just a random thought about a passed
loved one that pops into your head. You may find
yourself thinking of that person for no apparent
reason. That's spirit asking to be let in. Anything
that makes you stop for a split second, grabs your
attention and makes you think "what was that,
I just saw something", is probably a sign. It can
range from a little nudge from spirit to a big elbow
in the ribs. Sometimes they can give you a physical
sign. You could be thinking of your departed mum
and a white feather drifts down in front of you.
You could be thinking about your grandfather all
day and there will be a little Robin there in the garden when you get home that has never been there
before sitting and looking at you. Signs are ways
that spirit will make your brain stop and think. To
do this spirit uses the energy that connects us all,
living and dead.

I am sure some spirits have more energy than
others because of the different level of detail I get
from messages when I am on stage. Some come
through with a barrage of accurate information
which is recognised by someone in the audience

immediately. Others are sparse and connect to no one, most likely because the detail is too scant or because the person in the audience does not want to take the message for one reason or another. And just as some spirits are stronger than others, the ability to connect also varies between individuals on Earth plane. Some people come back to my shows five times. They go to different theatres and get a message from each. They can be in Tunbridge Wells and get a message from their dearly departed mum and the next year be in Croydon and get a message from their great grandfather. It's like a dance, all the elements have to line up and be synchronised and some people are better rehearsed and have more natural rhythm than others.

I am fascinated by how the process works. I know that one of the keys is our thought connection to the dead. In so many shows I host, people who receive messages have told me that they have been thinking about the person who comes through on the day of the show. Sometimes that thought may have been a few hours before, sometimes actually in the auditorium. Sometimes it is instant. There have been instances where a message comes through so strongly, just a single name, and I shout that name out – it is so loud in my head it makes me jump and I, in turn make the audience jump. Someone in the audience will shriek because it is their name I am calling and in the instant I call it they are thinking about the person in spirit who is channelling energy to them through me. They are ringing the doorbell to heaven and the person they are ringing for opens the door wide open.

When I get something right and the person I am reading for is touched by the details they hear I immediately feel we are connected. It is like a key in a lock. Some keys fit into different locks but there is only one which can be opened and when that message reaches the right person all the tumblers fall into place and the door to the afterlife opens.

Spirits work like safe-crackers. They fiddle with the combination to narrow down a message until it is recognisable to the correct receiver and the door opens. For example, I may have a message from a man in spirit named Paul and three people in the audience will put up their hands. I then get given further information; perhaps Paul died in a car crash, I then get his age or his address. Messages fill out like crossword puzzles until they are complete. There are little pieces of them and they all fit together. Sometimes they overlap or the pieces don't quite fit. The details often become increasingly specific. Other times I will get a rush of information all at once and it will be so specific it only makes sense to the one person in the audience it is meant for. Spirits know exactly who their messages are meant for and who they want to speak too.

Some people are more susceptible to certain types of signs than other.

Since a child I have always received names. I do not know why, but that seems to be what they give me to begin with before they widen out the content. But it always seems to start with a name. I suppose this is because spirits know names are the easiest and quickest way to get recognition. That's how you get attention in the first instance on Earth plane and the most effective way so perhaps that carries over to spirit.

When spirits come through they do not communicate with sounds as we humans do. The process transcends language. It is hard to explain in a way which makes sense completely. I often say I am spoken to by spirit and that spirit talks to me because it is easier to understand in those terms. But when I hear them it is not like a voice, it is like a word in my mind. It is a thought pattern. I might pick up the energy of a man in spirit and know he had a really deep voice with a Scottish accent but I don't hear his voice. I have a thought in my head and from that I know how he sounded. It is a bizarre process because I even think like they would have spoken when they were alive. A very poignant example of this happened a while ago when I picked up the energy of a little girl.

She was just 18 months old when she died. My mind was flooded with thoughts that I relayed directly to the audience. There was a name and in my mind I could see the girl. She was sitting in a highchair. Her grandmother was standing over her panicking. The thoughts that she was conveying to me were telling me that this was her death scene.

A lady in the audience stood. She was the little girl's mother. She confirmed all the details. Her daughter, Annabelle – the name I had been given – had died in the family kitchen aged 18 months while sitting in a highchair as her grandmother tried to save her.

'She got her toes stuck?' I asked.

The phrase was looping through my mind. Toes stuck, toes stuck. I couldn't quite work out what the girl was trying to communicate.

'Did she get caught in the chair?' I wondered. Perhaps the girl had fallen and been injured I guessed.

Her mother explained.

'She choked to death,' she said sadly, 'she was eating toast and it got caught in her throat.'

The little girl wasn't telling me her *toes* got stuck, she was telling me her *toast* got stuck, but because she was young and had such a limited vocabulary, that was how she was explaining it; toast stuck. After all a child wouldn't say 'I choked to death', a child would say 'my toast got stuck'.

When spirits communicate it often goes beyond words. I sometimes get flooded with their personality and take on facets of the way they appeared as well as their vocabulary. If they were stooped I will feel myself hunching over. I feel what they felt through the process of thought. It's like little bits of their energy connect with my mind. I become a psychic puppet. They give me their feelings as signs.

Since I've been on tour, the sense and feeling of how people passed has become far greater. There have been times when the feelings were so strong they would manifest themselves physically. I have had marks on my hands and arms; little scratches and bruises that relate to someone passing. It is not scary and the spirit doesn't mean to harm me. It is more a case that in those moments the energy is so strong it leaves a mark. But since I have been doing the tour I really get a sense of what they were feeling like when they passed. I suppose it is because of the concentration of energy in the room.

Sometimes they give clues as to what signs to look for. At a show on the South coast I was linked to a woman in spirit. She spoke quietly, there was a sense of urgency in her message, as if she was under some form of time constraint as was about to leave quickly. The message came through for someone on the same row as the message before. The first name I got was Claire.

'Who is Claire?' I asked.

'That's me,' the lady replied. I had her mother in spirit.

'She says here,' I explained, pointing at my chest. 'I don't feel like my breast is there.'

The lady nodded.

'I had breast cancer after my mother passed.'

I told her that her mother was with her and that she had known all about her daughter's illness. I saw redness, in my mind, like a wound. I told the lady in the audience.

'I had reconstruction,' she confirmed.

I felt urge to gag, as if there was a pressure building up in my chest that needed to be released. I could feel a sense of agitation; my body language mirrored that of the lady who was coming through to me from spirit when she died. Again, there was urgency, as if time was running out.

'At the very end of her life there was a panic. She knew that it was the end but it happened so quickly,' I said.

'It was very sudden,' the lady confirmed.

The connection started to fade and as it did I was shown what sign the lady in spirit would give her daughter in the future to let her know she was there.

'You will get a sense of your mum,' I explained. 'This sounds a little bit disconcerting but it may be that you can't swallow properly. That is the sense of your mum, that's how you will know she is there.' Sometimes there's no logic to the signs they chose!

Smells can be another sign we are given, as in the case of Ilene, a spirit who came through at a show in East Anglia. She showed me the scene of her death, to validate her message. She was lying sprawled, half on and half off a bed. It was a powerful message, very vivid. My mind took me to the scene. I was in her room and I could smell her. I told the receiver.

'Yeah you would be able to smell her,' she laughed. 'We could always smell her.'

At the same show another spirit came to me and the first sense I got was smell. His name was Brian and he gave me the name Christine. A lady took the message. Brian was her brother, Christine was her sister-in-law.

'He's very whiffy,' I apologised. She laughed and nodded.

'Brian's apologising. One of the signs you'll get when he comes to you is that you'll think someone has let one rip! You'll think: "who did that?" It will be Brian. He had a really bad tummy.'

She nodded again.

'He smells like John does occasionally,' I joked.

To the outsider, it can sometimes seem that the messages spirits give are horrific and disturbing. This is because inevitably the details are bound up with the details of their deaths. At one show I was giving a reading for a lady when suddenly, out of the blue, a horrific scene popped into my mind.

I gasped mid-sentence.

'I don't want to see that,' I reeled.

I picked up the name of the victim. He was being killed by a group of men who were beating his feet and legs. I also got the sense that there was a link to South Africa.

I gave the message as I received it.

'He is dark, very tall and very gentle. He was murdered by three men,' I said.

The message meant nothing to the lady who I had been talking too. Another spirit had come in. A few seats away I saw a hand rise tentatively. I screamed. I didn't want to go through with what was obviously a violent and sickening death. But I knew I had to.

A very normal woman stood up, not the type who looked like she would know anything about a murder. She stood with another woman. I told her I had someone in spirit who had been tortured to death. She said yes, she knew what I was talking about but that it didn't happen in South Africa, it happened in Nepal. The victim had travelled from South Africa before his death. She also confirmed that he had been beaten by three people who held him down and broke all the bones in his feet.

'Was he black,' I asked. The man I saw was very dark.

She shook her head. Then it became clearer. He was burnt, his body was charred. She confirmed that after his death his body was placed on a funeral pyre. His flesh was blackened. The man showing himself was not highlighting the gruesome details of his death to scare or unsettle anyone. He was offering the details so the lady could be sure it was him.

Three years ago I started to recognise and understand that when someone stood to take a message, if they stood with another person the energy felt stronger. The more people who stood together, the more accurate and detailed the messages seemed to be. Multiple people amplified the energy connection. I noticed this by accident. I first started asking people to stand together because I am a touchy-feely, tactile person and I thought that if it was me in the audience getting an emotional message from a loved one I would want someone to hold my hand. I would feel more supported and confident in front of a room full of strangers. But I started to realise that when two people are connected and they are in a spiritual situation, they are attracting more energy. They are plugs in a psychic power socket and the more plugs you have, the more energy comes through. And the clearer the connection, the easier it is for me to read the information that comes through. For this reason I'll often ask people to speak up as when I can hear them clearly, so can spirit. The pathway connects better if someone is open and engaged in what's going on. It's not a case of me reading body language as sceptics will claim. It is about clarity. The more people involved the better. At one show three girls stood together holding hands and the message was incredible. As they all stood up I got everything. It rushed in. They were near the front and I could see them clearly. They were all vocal and they all wanted to talk. Their combined energy was strong. All the names and dates and details I was given by spirit were spot on. The spirit who came through for them was a member of their family who had died of cancer. After the show the girls queued up to see me and told me they were blown away by what I had given them. They explained that the previous day had been the anniversary of the death of the person who came through and that they had tried to get tickets a month ago but couldn't. They only rang up the venue on the off-chance of some returns the day before and got the last three tickets. There is no such thing as coincidence. They were meant to be at that show.

Can I learn to be psychic?

My psychic awakening happened when I was four. I remember very clearly around the age I started nursery I began to realise I was different. Before that there were lots and lots of little incidents but they were fleeting.

We all have a latent psychic ability which is our natural form of intuitiveness. That is the starting point of any gift, to be able to listen to what your spiritual side is telling you and to listen to your instincts. There are several trains of thought about how you can develop this further into what would be described as fully-fledged mediumship. There are people who feel they can teach it, there are people who think you can learn it from books. Personally I feel that natural mediums are born with a heighted gift and a purpose. I believe I was meant to be a medium, even though I thought I was going to be a midwife. That was my path right from the word go.

I don't believe I would have been able to practice the ability to the high level I do if I had learnt it from a course. To be able to operate at the top level you need some form of natural ability. But on another level, if you want to open yourself up to the psychic world and maybe sense spirit or be more aware and in tune with it, I think there are ways you can develop it. It must start from within you. It is about trusting your gut feeling. It's about recognising when you get an intuitive feeling, trusting it and acting on it. It's about learning to know what those intuitive feelings are. Sadly there are many elements on Earth plane which stop us from developing and trusting these feelings. Adults pass doubts and scepticism to children, which is a shame because children are incredibly psychic; many see things and have invisible friends. And we tell them not to be so silly and to grow up. We tend to kill off their psychic ability with kindness, suppressing it until it closes.

Many people believe meditation can help. For some people it becomes almost an art form. Through meditation they transcend to another place. And it certainly can affect the way your brain works. There have been scientific studies which show that regular meditation can help alter brain waves, so perhaps there really is something in it, perhaps it helps to clear the brain's psychic pathway and makes it easier to connect to spirit, like clearing a path through snow.

I have never had to meditate to do what I do. There have been times when I've sat down for some quiet time and made an effort to clear my mind but it never stays clear for long because it gets filled with messages.

Some mediums also have rituals and props they rely on. If it works for them, fine. Some have crystals and talismans. I'm not sure how that helps. In fact sometimes my back to basics approach confuses the wider psychic community. I once delivered a lecture at the College of Psychic Studies in London and when they ushered me in they told me that the "meditation room" was down the hall and was a place of peace and tranquillity where I could collect my thoughts.

'You want me awake don't you?' I laughed. 'If I sit in a quiet room I'll fall asleep.'

Instead I asked for a room with a TV. They seemed shocked.

There are people who think the only way you can recognise the signs of spirit are if you dress the process up in ceremony and hocus-pocus. I used to have a client who would come to see me when I worked from home and would walk through the office door and take off his shoes and socks so he could be grounded. He used to chant too. He wore big baggy trousers and sat in the lotus position. I used to wonder how that would affect what I was doing and he used to think I was missing out on something by not getting into what he perceived as a spiritual state of mind. If it works for you however and you feel it helps you communicate with spirit then why not?

On the other hand there is a train of thought that people who try too hard are pulling spirit to them rather than inviting it in and letting it come naturally. Personally I do not call spirit or wake them up or ask them to come to me. They come to me if they want to. The trick is to be open, rather than to chase.

I usually try and explain to the audiences in my shows that they can develop their ability in the hope that they will be able to experience some of the wonderful, comforting things I experience. I'm no different from anyone else. I am human. I am made of the same stuff; flesh and blood. It is just that my ability has been exercised all my life. Mainly unbeknown I have been developing it from a very early age.

You need to trust. It is not about a belief system. It is about trusting your gut feelings. It is about trusting in the signs that are all around you. Why not a white feather? Why not a Robin? Why not a smell or a touch? Everyone can experience these. It is about trusting that those gut feelings you have when you see or experience something you think may have an extra dimension to it actually is what you subconsciously feel it is; a message from spirit. If you give that credence, the spirit who sent it will come back and the next time they do their energy will be even stronger and the sign even more obvious. If you carry on like that you will develop your own psychic ability.

Is death a punishment?

No it certainly isn't because really there is no death. I know that sounds a bit crazy but hear me out. Our souls are eternal, they go on forever. They are the fundamental element of who we are, they are our essence and if the essence of who we are doesn't die, neither do we. Energy is eternal, it changes but it can neither be destroyed nor created. It has no beginning or end. When our body ceases to function, our soul goes on to another plane; another dimension. The only unpleasant part of death is what the body experiences sometimes and that is fleeting. As soon as our essence is released there is no pain because the soul detaches itself from the bodily form. Why do spirits come back and communicate details about the pain their bodies experienced in life? They do it for validation and to let their loved ones know they are no long in pain. The memory of it does not affect them. At the moment of bodily death they are released from the neurons and nerve endings that create pain. Often spirits illustrate this by showing themselves without the afflictions which beset them in life. I remember one such message vividly. The spirit of a man came through at a show in the North East and as I picked up his energy I could see an image of him in my mind's eye. He was standing in a living room next to a wheelchair. His hand was resting on the handle of the wheelchair and he was smiling. I initially wondered whether he had been a carer or a hospital porter during his physical life.

'I have a man here, he is in his fifties and his name is Graham,' I told the audience. I had picked up his name as soon as he came through. I explained about the wheelchair and started to describe him.

'He is tall; around six feet, and he has a distinctive tattoo on his forearm. It looks like a dragon.'

A young lady in the audience raised her hand.

'That's my uncle,' she said. More names came through and each of them related to a member of the lady's family or a friend of her uncle Graham.

'Was he a hospital porter?' I asked.

She shook her head.

'What's with the wheelchair then? What does it mean?'

'Uncle Graham was involved in a motorcycle accident when he was young. He broke his spine and was paralysed,' she explained. 'He never really recovered, he was wheelchair bound and had lots of problems with his health for the rest of his life.'

Although most of those who knew Graham would have recognised him in a wheelchair as that had defined him in his later years, he had chosen to show himself standing to let his family know that he was free from pain and to say "look, I am not longer constrained by my body". The point of this story is that death is not painful, it is beautiful and so it cannot be a punishment because punishment, by its very nature must in some way be uncomfortable or unpleasant. The ones who are really punished when someone dies are the ones who are left here on Earth to carry on with their lives without the person they loved. Spirits acknowledge this. They do not grieve but they recognise our grief and they feel our pain at their loss, which is why they have a need to show themselves and let us know they are with us.

That fact that death is not a punishment is still not an excuse to behave badly, however. We are punished for doing wrong but we have to think carefully about what really constitutes badness. Our idea of acceptable behaviour changes over time. In the Victorian age six and seven year old children who were starving and stole bread got sent to prison. Were they bad? Society changes and with it so does the concept of what is good and bad. Evil is a different kettle of fish. It is very real in the world. We can all think of evil people, such as Hitler. I grew up in the fifties and my parents told me about the Holocaust. That was utterly evil. There are genocides committed in places across the world and they are fuelled by evil energy. They are perpetrated by people who are evil. Although it seems hard to comprehend because souls are associated with good, these people do have souls. Their souls are tainted with evil energy however. I haven't fully worked out what happens to them yet but I do think somehow they are sent back to Earth as some form of punishment or to make amends and cleanse themselves. On the whole I believe evil stays in Earth as I have only ever encountered one evil spirit (more of that later).I have met mischievous ones who pull hair or say naughty things. When I was young we had a spirit in the house who would tell us to keep our records quiet and would shout at us when we played too loudly. He wasn't bad, he was mischievous and he certainly wasn't evil.

What are ghosts, why do they haunt things and are spirits and ghosts the same thing?

Ghosts are spirits which show themselves in a visual form. They use visual signs and manifestations because some people react better to visual stimulus. Others react better to sounds and some to smells. For example my eyes are terrible. I wear glasses and without them I am as blind as a bat. However, my sense of smell is very acute and in many cases a spirit will give me scent signs because they know smell is my strong sense. Spirits use their energy to show themselves in different ways depending on what the receiver will react best too. With me they also use taste. Again taste has always been one of my most heavily utilised senses and ever since I was little I have been tasting spirit! When I was a girl, I used to know I was about to have one of my "happenings" because I would get a metallic taste in my mouth. They do this because they want to be noticed and they want to create that connection between our world and theirs. It can be unpleasant. I had recently connected with one old boy while in stage and it was obvious he had wet himself. He showed me a scene which he hoped would register with someone in the audience. I saw him take his soiled trousers off and put them over a radiator to dry them off. I could see it in my mind and I could also smell it. Someone took the message because they knew who he was. They told me it was what he used to do and whenever they visited they would have to hold their nose. That was his signature smell.

When spirits appear visually as what we call ghosts or apparitions, they don't mean to scare us. We are not used to seeing them, it doesn't seem real when we do and usually it is so unexpected that initially we are frightened. We don't always get any warning.

A great example came to me at a show I did in the North. The message came from a card which was left for me at the show by a group of women. The card asked if Marlene had anything to say. She did. I picked up her spirit and was shown a mirror. It was an ornate hand mirror with a silver handle. I saw Marlene's face staring out of it. I knew instinctively what the message meant.

I told the group.

'One of you owns a mirror she used to have. I don't want to frighten you but what I am about to say could be seen as scary. You might see her in the mirror when you hold it up,' I told the group.

It sounded like a typical scene from a Hollywood spine-tingler; the ghostly image of a dead person appearing in an antique mirror.

One of the women in the group squealed.

'I've seen her through the mirror.'

I gasped.

'How mental is that! Did you scream?'

'I was shocked,' admitted the woman.

The mirror was obviously a sentimental object which allowed Marlene a portal to show herself. Sometimes spirits inhabit spaces on Earth plane that they had an emotional attachment too. That may not always be a good emotion but they are drawn to specific places. Sometimes they can seem random, almost bizarre.

At a show in Aberdeen I connected to the spirit of a woman, she gave me the names Susan and Jackie. I could see her clearly and she was in a car. I could also sense the energy of a gentleman in spirit with her. There was a loud noise. A man stood up to take the message and told me that Susan was a taxi driver who had died. Her friend at the firm was Jackie. He confirmed that he had been speaking about Susan before he came in to the auditorium.

'I think her spirit is in that car,' I explained. 'She is showing me it. And she is often around Jackie when she is at work.'

The noise I was hearing sounded like a crash and I was sure this was relevant to her untimely death. I explained this to the man and he explained that a few weeks before she died, Susan was in a collision with a bus and that afterwards she had never felt right.

The man in the audience went on to explain that her father was also in spirit; the older man she was with.

I told the man that Jackie needed to watch out

for signs of Susan in the car she used to drive as this is where she would show herself.

Another similar reading happened a few years ago when I had connected to a lady in spirit and she was showing me her walk to work. She was a teacher and lived close to the school she taught in. Each day she made the same journey and when she came through during a show in the West Country she showed me the route. She was showing me because one of her work colleagues was in the audience and it was the best way to validate the message. Her workmate recognised my description and took the message. I had felt her presence even before the show started. She knew that her former workmate was going to be at the venue.

I told the lady in the audience what I was picking up.

'Even today she has walked that route. In the nicest possible way the school you work in is haunted.'

People are entitled to be scared of ghosts because they come out of nowhere and then they disappear. Most of the time they appear out of curiosity. It's like someone saying hello or calling your name when you are not expecting it and you freak out and run away.

When they do appear and we can see them it is a real privilege. One of the most vivid apparitions I was privileged to see appeared many years agowhen I used to do one-to-one readings at my home. A lady was sitting with me and she wanted to contact the spirit of her husband. He came through so strongly an image of him appeared there in front of us. It was transparent and ephemeral, like a reflection in glass. She shrieked, I shrieked and she ran out the door. The image faded away, it dissipated like the vapour trails from an airplane high in the sky. She was left standing outside in the driveway. It took a while before I could coax her inside and convince her how lucky she had been. Her husband was so keen to contact her, his energy manifested itself in an image. The terms ghost and haunting have taken on negative meanings over the years but anyone who sees one is very lucky indeed.

Is there a God?

This is the same as asking if there is anything which controls the afterlife. The answer I believe is yes. There is some form of guiding energy, some would call this God but God means different things to different denominations. In my view God, if you want to call it something, is the guardian energy; the source of all love and divinity; it's the power station that radiates and attracts pure psychic energy – the mother ship. As far as I am concerned I really have a problem with religion saying that if you want to feel God and know God you have to follow a prescribed faith system or belief system. I disagree completely. It is lovely to go to church and sing and be part of a community. I was bought up as a Christian in the Church of England and went to church three or four times a week and I loved it when I was little. I still love Songs of Praise and I live in an old rectory next door to a church. But I don't feel close to God because of that. I like the idea of being part of a community which is fundamentally based on doing good but I don't think going to church will connect me to the concept of God any more than going to the library or the supermarket will. There are no short cuts. You don't have to be psychic to talk to God. Anyone can,

God is within us, it is a spirit and energy like we are. There are days when I sense God. I might have done something good and feel a warm glow inside. That is God reminding me it is here. Other times I may have done something not so nice; maybe when I have been horrible to John. I feel a twinge of guilt. That's God nudging me and reminding me to be good. I know that mother ship dwells within me and I am no different to anyone else so it dwells in all of us. Maybe God is our conscious. The God I envisage does not judge sternly and does not demand people jump through hoops to be good and spiritual, you either are good on the whole or you are not. The God I envisage allows people to make mistakes because that is how we learn. We are all on a journey and we have a destination but we can all go different ways around it and in order to be able to empathise and have compassion we have to be in situations where we make mistakes so we can understand what it means to be fallible. Mistakes strengthen character and soul. Getting nearer to God is about learning lessons and getting over hurdles. It is not about following a set of rules. There is no rule book that says you have to be good for ten lifetimes; there is no doctrine or dogma. Goodness gets recognised but it does not matter in what actions it has manifested itself. You could have helped a friend when you were five and shared a sweet. You could have stood in front of a bus and prevented it from hitting a child when you were 30. They are both good acts and both treated equally. There are no scores. Getting closer to divinity is about deeds and the way you conduct yourself through life. It's about whether you have generally been a decent human being, shown respect and loved and been open and embraced life and I think we have to have more than one lifetime to hone that goodness to the point where we are allowed into divinity.

This Godly higher energy calls us to it when we die. If we have enough goodness and love we are let in, if we haven't we come back for another go. Another way of looking at it is that divinity is the hive and we are the bees. We go out into Earth plane for a while, collect love, and then when we die we are called back to it where we become part of the whole. All energy in the hive is connected, like atoms in a body, separate but integral in a single entity.

God, or the divine place, is the root of everything. In our realm science says that everything came from the big bang. All the known matter in the universe was created at that instant. We are all made of the universe; we are all made of stardust. The matter that makes our bodies assembles to form us and when we die all those atoms disassemble and go off to make something else. Why shouldn't something similar happen in the spirit realm. Why shouldn't our energy come from a single event and place, inhabit us, leave us when we die and go on to form part of something else?

There are a lot of people who don't believe in

God or the afterlife and because of that they don't care about ever reaching a higher state after death. The good news for them is that they'll get there because God isn't a being and doesn't judge, it doesn't care whether you believe in it or not. It is there whether you light candles and chant about it or whether you never give it a thought in your life. I am not belittling religion or faith or belief systems. There are a lot of people who call themselves mediums or seers who really feel that they are only able to do what they do because they believe in God in the traditional sense but I think God is more complex and more fundamental than a lot of doctrines make out.

What creates psychic phenomenon?

Love is the key. It is the factor that lubricates the links between our world and the next. Love has everything to do with spirit because love nourishes psychic energy and so psychic events become much more probable when there is an element of love in the mix.

Even though in most of the messages I receive I don't know the spirit so I don't have a loving bond with him or her, the receiver of the message does and that is why the spirit will come through. It is drawn to me by the link of love.

When ghosts show themselves it is usually because they are in a place they loved or near someone they loved.

They often show themselves or send us signs in times of need or turmoil and again, this is because they love us. There are times in our lives when we are more open to contact from spirit and that is often when we are most vulnerable or at a cross-road in life. They come to guide us and to offer us support. Sometimes in the middle of our darkest times they swoop in to save us. Incredible things can happen when spirit intervenes.

A recent example happened when I was performing in Australia. I was at a show in a place called

Twin Towns. The evening started with amazing accuracy. A young man in spirit came to me and in my head I heard the word 'butter'. It was surreal. He told me that was his name was Brian and that he was 23. He also gave me the name Sonia.

'Does that make sense to anyone,' I asked the audience. No one took the message. More spirits came through. A lady called Jenny came through, she had passed suddenly. She gave me the name Julie.

At that point a lady stood in the audience to take the message. She explained that her grandmother in spirit was called Jenny, she lost a daughter when she was younger. The girl was called Julie. Her brother was called Brian, he had died at 23. She also had a granddaughter called Sonia.

The audience cheered.

I still wondered where butter fitted in though.

'I'm fascinated by the mention of butter – what does it mean?' I asked.

'It was Lurpak butter,' the lady explained. 'Every time when went to nana's she we would ask for butter in our mashed potato.'

I then received a message from a man who had died in a motorbike accident. His name was JD. A man in audience again confirmed all the details. I could feel the energy getting stronger and stronger and began to feel that it was building to something wonderful.

The next spirit came through and gave me details so specific and clear the message was taken straight away.

'I have the name Sheila and the surname Collins. This woman in spirit was called Shelia Collins and she died because of problem with her head,' I recounted. 'There may be someone here in the audience who saw her spirit recently.'

The woman who stood to take the first message stood again.

'My grandmother in spirit was Sheila Collins. She died of a brain tumour.' The audience gasped.

I was intrigued to get to the bottom of why I was sensing that Sheila had shown herself recently.

'Have you or anyone in your family felt they have seen her recently,' I asked.

The lady explained: 'I had a stroke in 2011 and since I woke from intensive care I have been able to see everything and anything but have never been able to see my nana until now. I can see her on the stage with you.'

She was overcome with emotion.

She continued.

'I don't know whether she thought it was too much for me but I was seeing everybody else's loved ones in spirit but not my own.'

I was gobsmacked.

Afterwards I had time to think about it. I realised what the implications were. In her darkest hour the lady was close to death and when she was lying in a coma, the spirits of her loved ones came to her and filled her with their energy. When she awoke she had been given a gift; the ability to see spirit so they would always be with her. Love made that possible.

Another factor that helps to grease the wheels of psychic wonder is curiosity. If you are curious and open to the realm of spirit they will reciprocate. They want to come through to us and show themselves. They are driven by curiosity too. As I have mentioned before, they can have an almost child-like sense of mischief and they are drawn to happy, inquisitive energy. If you are good humoured and trusting, you are more likely to see their signs. I believe that to be a good medium you need the right personality. You need to trust spirit, you need to be interested in people and their stories and you need a good sense of humour. If you have those attributes and love linking to spirit you are well-equipped for psychic adventures.

What happens when we grieve?

First we need to know what grief is. It is more than an emotion. It is pain and it is physical. Our body actually feels the loss of the loved one we grieve for.

There are different forms of love. There is the love we have for our friends which is different from the love we feel for our children or our partners. Grief for any of these can still be as intense as for the other. It can be so intense it is debilitating. For example, when a couple have been together for 40 or 50 years they have merged, they have become one. When one part of that relationship dies, the survivor has lost half of his or her being.

Grief is the body crying out and reacting to the loss of a loved one and yearning for that person. It is common to try and comfort someone suffering from grief by telling them that things will get better with time. Often they do, but the grief never goes, it just changes. In some circumstances it remains acute for the rest of that person's life, as in the case of a parent who has lost a child. They feel as if they have had their heart ripped out of their chest and years later at intervals when they are reminded of their loss, grief will return for periods and be as painful as ever. Grief is the price we pay for loving someone. It might change its appearance and the way it affects you but it never goes. It is a permanent reminder of loss. It sounds like a cruel statement but those suffering from grief need to realise that they will never get over it. You can't cheat grief. If you love someone and they die the fact is you are going to suffer. When people suffer from bereavement they look for answers, they clutch at everything. Tragically nothing can be done to bring back that person in the form they are used too.

There is a pattern to grief. It presents itself in stages which are individual to each person and each circumstance. There will be shock, there will be anger, there will be guilt. Sometimes there is even a stage of euphoria, where a person's body kicks into survival mode and they go through a period of denial. Grief totally changes your personality. It can make you numb and it is hard to cope with. The brain can go into shutdown mode to prevent you from literally losing your mind.

On a biological level some animal species have also been observed to mourn their dead. Although animal behaviourists have traditionally shied away from attributing human-like emotions to animals, creatures as diverse as dolphins, dogs and apes have all been seen to appear grief-stricken. Elephants have been observed staying with the body of a deceased elephant for long periods of time, like a two-year-old African elephant at a zoo in Hungary who stayed with its mother for 14 hours after she died. Keepers say the calf continued to weep after his mother's body was removed.

Similar behaviour was seen in 2008 when a gorilla at a German zoo mourned the death of her three-month-old baby. She carried his body around for almost a week and refused to let anyone take the baby away.

Many people, especially men, grieve in secret. They are embarrassed by the fact that they suffer uncontrollable waves of emotion that totally consume them. Part of that natural process is the irresistible urge to shed tears and most men don't like to cry in front of people so they do their grieving in private. It is not healthy. Over the last few decades I have seen more women fall victim to this secret grieving process. Many women hold down high-pressured jobs and come to rely on them as a crutch when they are bereaved, especially if they lose a partner. They go back to work too soon after their loss and feel they can not show emotion and vulnerability at work. They are driven to grieve on their own because of what society expects from women nowadays. They put on a mask to the outside world and keep a lid on their true emotions. The pressure builds all day until they get home and as soon as they are on their own the lid comes off. They are hit by a tidal wave of emotion and break down. Some turn to alcohol to try and deaden the pain but as it is a depressants, it exacerbates the problem.

Grief has so many negative effects. It affects

appetite. Grieving people tend to develop un-healthy relationships with food, either eating too little or comfort eating too much of the wrong food. It deprives people of sleep. They wake throughout the night and each time they do they are hit by the realisation they have lost a loved one and the pain become fresh again. Grief is exhausting.

We have rituals to help us cope with grief. Fu-nerals are part of the grieving process. They allow some form of closure and they confirm to those left behind that the person who has died will not be coming back in their bodily form. Funerals are so important because they give us the opportunity to say a formal goodbye to the earthly body and to respect the dead. They also provide a focus in the early days after a death. The organisation of a funeral gives the bereaved breathing space.

Grief can appear selfish. It happens because we miss the person who has passed and we crumble because they are not there. We think of our loss, not theirs. In my opinion this is right because the person who has died has gone on to a much better place and is happy there. Spirits don't want us to grieve. It saddens them to see us so distressed and they can't understand it because they are at rest and at peace in a wonderful place. That's why they want to come back and make contact. They want to tell us to stop being so silly and to show us they are still with us. That is the biggest consolation any grieving person can have; validation that the person they loved is safe, happy, at peace and still with them.

How can I cope with bereavement?

I recently spent the weekend with a very good friend who was widowed. I found the situation difficult because although I work with bereaved people every day and become emotionally involved in the readings I give them, they are strangers. Our paths only cross momentarily and although I empathise with them, I am not involved in their grief beyond the restrictions of our interaction. Dealing with my friend and her bereavement was different. I was not there to give her a reading or to try and put her in touch with her husband. I made a conscious decision long ago not to use my gift in that way because I do not believe it was given to me to use on a personal level. Instead I sat with my friend and tried to support and comfort her while she cried and tried to handle the waves of emotions that were threatening to swamp her. Tears are one of the first signs we show when we grieve and her tears were raw. She had lost her husband a month before and she was still in shock. In that respect grief is like an onion, there are lots of layers. You peel one layer off, go through one emotion and think nothing can be as bad as that and you hope that doesn't come back and then another emotion kicks in and there is this other layer. By its very nature, grief is confusing. People fear it.

As I sat there holding my friend's hand trying to make her think of the happy memories she shared with her husband it struck me that if I had put my medium hat on, it would have seemed inappropriate. While many people come to see my shows because they are grieving and hope to get a message, I wouldn't recommend that anyone in those first raw throes of grief go and seek out a medium because we are at our most vulnerable when we've recently lost someone. People looking for mediums are looking for reassurance that their loved one is okay. They want answers and they want contact; where has he gone, I can't remember his voice, what colour was his hair. They panic that the memories will fade too quickly. We take it all for granted when our loved ones are alive and we see them every single day.

We also fear they are suffering so we want validation that they are in Heaven or the afterlife and at peace. A good medium can do this but bereaved people should wait until they are emotionally resilient enough to seek out this validation. The process may take months or sometimes years. I always feel that the people who come to me are meant to be there and that in many cases they come because spirit orchestrates it. I have had so many occasions where the people who get messages at my show explain that they are only there because of random circumstances; they booked for the wrong show or they bought tickets on a whim. This is spirit guiding them.

A reading from an accurate, reputable medium can be an enriching, rewarding experience and can give a huge boost of hope in the throes of bereavement but I urge caution. A bad experience can push you deeper down into your grief and can damage any recovery you have made. If the spirit of the person you are desperate to contact fails to come through you feel rejection. I struggle with the knowledge that I can never give messages to everyone in the audiences of my shows. It saddens me but there is nothing I can do about it. Usually there are over 1000 people in the audience and I know many of them are there because they want a message. It's simple mathematics to work out that many of them will go away disappointed although my hope is that by witnessing the messages I do pass on, those that don't connect with their loved ones will get validation that wonderful things do happen and that our loved ones are there in spirit.

Some people make plans to cope with bereavement before the death of a loved one by making pre-arrangements. I have met people who are terminally ill and who tell their loved ones to seek out a medium after their death so they can make a connection. They have pre-planned signs and words. They even arrange to meet in places that hold special memories. Inevitably the person listening will say "don't be silly, don't talk like that, you are not going to die". In a way they are right. Death is not the end. When a loved one dies we have memories and they are not wiped out. They survive for a reason. They are the links we have with our departed loved ones. We can pull on them and in pulling on them we bring that person back to us. A thought is a prayer, we pray for them to be there. When the body dies only the body dies. You've had all that time with that person to create memories and the memories will bring the soul of your departed back to you. Use them in times of need and get comfort from them.

For those who feel overwhelmed by grief after bereavement there are amazing grief counselling services out there. Cruse is a national bereavement support charity which helps anyone of any age.

And you should never be afraid to talk about the person you are grieving for. Never be afraid to go to bed with their nightie or their t-shirt or wear their perfume or cuddle something that belonged to them so you can feel closer to them. My mother was only 21 when she lost her mum. Before that they were inseparable and she grieved all her life. As a little girl I remember mum used to cuddle this pink nightie that belonged to my Gran and kept it until it became completely threadbare. She only ever hand washed it to stop it wearing away. When it eventually had to be thrown away because it was just fine gossamer, she was devastated. Others don't want to remember because there is so much pain associated with remembering, but usually remembering can give comfort, especially if you concentrate on the good things. Do not dwell on the bad and the negative; it doesn't help the flow of energy. Remember the fun and the laughs you had with your loved ones.

Can spirits help me find love?

Nothing knows the value of love more than spirit. It thrives on love and it wants us to have as much love in our lives as we possibly can. And for that reason spirit will often show us the way when it comes to matters of the heart. Man has known this for hundreds of years, assigning those sudden feelings and hunches we get about prospective partners as arrows from Cupid's bow. Love intuition has been represented as being controlled by otherworldly beings such as Eros or Aphrodite the Goddess of love. Although we chose who we fall in love with based on a whole host of conscious and subconscious decisions and information, there is definitely a spiritual element, especially when couples meet by chance. People who are meant to be together are brought together by a higher power. Unbeknown to them they are introduced by spirit which acts as a celestial dating agency; a sort of match.com from the afterlife!

Spirit world provides many signs and pointers when it comes to finding love and the secret is to learn to listen to what it is saying. And that means following your gut and your heart, rather than your head.

First impressions are very powerful and often

they prove right because we make snap judgements about people we meet based on a whole host of unconscious clues. Those first impressions are unclouded by conscious information and are often spot on. They are informed by our intuition and our intuition feeds our psychic ability. Spirit will send signs that come in the form of gut feeling and instinct and they give pure unbiased advice because they want the best for us. Ultimately it is down to us to make decisions about who we chose to fall in love with and we usually do this with our brains. However, sometimes our brain and the judgement it creates are clouded by past experience, whereas spirit has no ulterior motives. We may pass over the chance of dinner with a work colleague because he looks like a former lover even if we feel a link and an attraction to that person. Spirit is telling us one thing, and our brains are telling us another. Go with spirit. It knows best.

It is all about trust. If we trust and know they are there, they will help us. Spirit doesn't want us to be lonely. It wants to enrich our lives.

You should also never be afraid to ask spirit for a sign and for guidance. It will answer. If you have lost a loved one and have moved on in your grief to the point where you are ready to start another relationship but are worried that you will upset the person you lost, ask. I have never come across a spirit yet who was not pleased when a loved one moved on and found love again. Jealousy does not exist in the afterlife. If our instinct tells us it is the right thing to do we should listen because that is a sign. We should also watch out for other signs because spirit is always watching. They help us find not only love, but other things we have lost. Every week I give messages to people to direct them to items and people they have lost. Sometimes they help reunite people with family members they have lost touch with, other times they recover lost or stolen objects.

At a recent show I picked up a spirit named Greg. I could sense he wanted to contact a woman in the audience for a specific reason, rather than just to say "hello".

Several images popped into my mind. I could visualise a car. It was a silver hatchback and I instinctively knew it was Greg's car. I also saw a gold necklace. The car and the jewellery were linked in some way. I picked up the name Sarah.

I relayed all the information to the audience and a woman raised her hand. Her name was Sarah and she had lost a friend called Greg who owned a silver hatchback.

'Did you lose a necklace in the car?' I asked.

She nodded her head. After Greg's death another man had taken the car. He was a member of Greg's family but was not a nice person. Sarah had never been given the opportunity to recover her necklace because the man would not let her search in the car. She suspected he'd found it and kept it for himself.

Greg knew all this and was incensed by the

injustice of it. But he had words of comfort. I told Sarah what Greg was telling me.

'The person who now has the car will not give the necklace back but he will get seven months in prison and when he does that's when you will be able to recover your necklace,' I told her.

The woman gasped. She was dumbstruck. Everything I said made perfect sense to her. The man was indeed awaiting sentencing for a crime he had committed. Greg was letting her know so she could recover her sentimental jewellery.

How do I forgive someone who is dead and do the dead forgive us?

Forgiveness is a theme that comes up repeatedly in my work because it is associated with guilt and guilt is one of the primary emotions that people feel after the death of a loved one. Guilt is an unpleasant but natural reaction when we lose someone. Did we do enough for them, were we there for them, did we love them enough? These are just a few of the common questions that tumble over and over in the minds of people who have been bereaved. And because they feel guilty, they often seek forgiveness.

Looking after elderly and sick people towards the end of their lives is always fraught with emotional and moral issues and none more so than when children decide that their parents need to be cared for in a home. Often the parent is reluctant and that leaves a deep sense of guilt.

We live in an age where people are living longer and are increasingly being kept alive after suffering serious conditions such as strokes and heart attacks. Children have to make the heartbreaking decision to place a parent in a home, sometimes separating them from an elderly spouse. The situation also inevitably arises when a parent suffers from Alzheimer's disease. In these cases the children are faced with a difficult choice. They either look after the parent themselves, which can be incredibly stressful and demanding, or they can place them in a nursing home.

During my stage shows I invite audience members to leave cards with messages on. These can act as a social barometer which gives an indication of the types of issues people are concerned with; asking for forgiveness from parents is possibly the most common theme. Questions such as "did they understand why they were in a home" and "were they unhappy" are posed nightly.

One such card at a recent show read: "Does she forgive me for putting her in a home."

I could sense that the card was soaked in emotion. The lady who wrote it had tortured herself wondering whether her mother, who had passed, hated her for making the decision. As I read it out I sensed the mother in spirit. She was there with me, smiling gently and looking out across the audience to her daughter. All signs of the dementia that had tainted her last years had been washed away and she showed herself to me as she would have appeared in her earlier life. She was serene and at peace. I heard her voice in my head. 'There is nothing to forgive,' it whispered. I could feel the energy of love reaching out across the rows of seats. The lady in the audience who had written the card stood.

I told her that her mother was with her and that she understood why the decision had to be made.

'We all make choices and decisions that, given

another time and place, we would perhaps make differently. But to have even asked this question shows that you loved your mum,' I explained.

'You have your family and your responsibilities now. Your mum was taken care of. She was at a time of her life where it wasn't really bothering her and you chose carefully for her.'

I hope my words put her mind at rest.

To us death seems so final. Many believe it marks the last time we are able to communicate with our loved ones and so anything left unsaid remains unsaid. This is particularly hard when people are estranged and one dies or when the last contact they had was an argument. They never had the chance to say sorry and make up and they worry that the ill feelings will be the last thing the dead person remembered about them before dying.

But spirits do communicate with us and we can forgive them as they forgive us. Ill feelings do not pass into the afterlife. Death is like a barrier which lets love and energy through but holds back negative feelings.

An example of this happened at a show in Wales. The soul of lady came to me. She gave me names and dates and a lady in the audience took the message and explained that the woman in spirit was her sister, Jeanette.

Jeanette was showing me a far away land and a man there. I felt a family connection between the two. I asked the lady in the audience what the significance of this imagery was and she explained.

'We have a brother in Australia,' she said.

Jeanette was sending this man a message. She wanted him to know that she was sorry and that she had always loved him and that he mustn't feel sad.

I asked the lady in the audience what the significance of this message was.

'Before he emigrated they had an argument and they never patched things up,' she said.

Jeanette had come back to let her brother know that she loved him.

'She is at peace now and wants you to know that her energy is everywhere. She is buzzing around everyone, she visits him often,' I said.

Although bad feelings do not pass over, sometimes spirits who have done bad things on Earth feel the need to repent in death and come back to ask for forgiveness from their loved ones. Why is this? I have a feeling it is to redress the balance between good and bad and to cleanse their energy. Perhaps they get sent back by the divine energy to make amends.

I have experienced a few such messages and each time the feeling I get from the energy that comes through is unsettling. The most recent example happened at a show in the Home Counties.

I was giving a message to a lady in the audience. The spirit was a lady, she was with twin babies. As I was relaying details from her the energy of a man came through. Violent images suddenly rushed through my mind.

'I have a man here too,' I explained. 'He's done

something terrible. I have a bad feeling about this one. This man did a very long prison sentence.'

He had come in to apologise for what he did. I was sweating. I was given names; Margaret and Michael. The message made no sense to the lady who had taken the earlier message but another woman stood up. Her brother, Michael, died from a blow to the back of the head and her mother, Margaret, died from a brain tumour.

'You haven't got a link to someone who did something really bad have you?' I asked.

She was a rough diamond. Her voice was harsh, like she'd smoked too many fags.

'I know a few big men in prison. It's all connected to my father. If I told you who he was you'd understand. He did 25 years,' she said cryptically.

My blood ran cold.

The message was very clear.

'Did he pass in prison,' I shivered.

'Yes,' she confirmed. 'I'm glad he's dead really.'

'He's come through because he wants forgiveness. He keeps saying he is sorry.'

Michael was there too and I got the feeling that he wanted to mediate.

'He wants everything to be ok,' I told her.

Michael also showed me a young man who was deaf in one ear and who was thinking of taking up boxing again after a break. The lady confirmed her nephew had a perforated eardrum which he had received in the ring.

And the reading got even more shocking. I

sensed a girl and the name Sarah. The woman nodded sadly and said she was Sarah's godmother.

'It's another tragic tale,' she said. 'I saw you a few
years ago and you came through with the same
message. You had a Sarah and she was locked in a
van. I didn't take the message that time. I was too
scared. She was found in the woods.'

The woman went on to explain that the little girl
I was picking up was Sarah Payne, the little girl
who was abducted and murdered in 2000. It was a
tragic and very high profile case. Sarah was seven
when she was snatched by paedophile Roy Whit-
ing near her grandparent's home in West Sussex.
He held her in his white van before murdering her.

This lady had certainly faced hard times in her
life and had suffered tragedy. The spirit of her father recognised this and wanted to make amends.

Anyone who murders someone else has some bad
in them but there are murders that happen without
intent. There are people who have killed for reasons
they believe are just, look at soldiers, it is their job.
Are they deserving of forgiveness? I believe yes they
are for our own sense of humanity. And then there
are people who are beyond forgiveness and in that
instance the higher energy will sort that out. There
has to be justice here on Earth because we all live
together in a harmonious and civilised way and for
the worst offenders there are implications.

Does my pet have a soul?

Animals not only have souls, they are also psychic. Their energy is pure because they haven't been tainted and they are much more in tune with instinct and intuition than humans are.

Anyone who owns a cat or a dog will know what I'm talking about. I know my three bulldogs are psychic. They see spirits all the time. I live in an old rectory full of psychic energy and they pick up on it. They can be lying there, snoozing away when suddenly they'll sit bolt upright, look intently at what appears to be empty space and then run off chasing something that isn't there to the untrained eye.

Animals come back after they die. I have seen all sorts since I was a little girl including dogs, cats and even a seal! They give pure unconditional love because their energy is pure and they want to keep connected to those they love in death as well as in life.

I've had dogs all my life. Several years before my bulldogs I had Holly who was five when she was run over and died. I loved her and went to pieces for a week after the accident. I was so grief-stricken I stayed in bed and couldn't work. In the depths of my despair she came to comfort me. It was early in the morning. I'd cried myself to sleep the night before and dreamt vividly about her all that night. The dreams were her signs to me. I was just waking up and as I opened my eyes I saw her face looking down at me. She was sitting on my chest staring at me. I blinked, confused at first. For a split second I thought maybe her death had been a terrible dream. I cried her name and went to stroke her but my hand went straight through the apparition. It was beautiful to know that her spirit was there with me but still so sad because she was dead. I cried as the image faded and I still well up with emotion when I remember it.

Our animals go to the same place we do. I believe that we elevate them and enrich their souls in life because we love them so much. They are attuned to us. Have you ever noticed how they mirror your moods? If you are happy, your dog is happy. If you are down they seem down. It makes me feel guilty when I think about what we do to them. We have them castrated or neutered! Thankfully they love us unconditionally so they forgive. They come back from the vet minus a few important parts and they still love us.

They understand more than we realise. My dogs know when I am going away on tour and they get upset. They listen to me and John talking and they get miserable and sit there looking at me accusingly with their big eyes. I don't even have to bring my suitcase down the stairs, they just know. They sense it.

Anyone who doubts that dogs love their owners only has to read the story of Greyfriars Bobby, the loyal police hound. According to reports he belonged to Constable John Gray who served in the Scottish police force in the mid 19th Century and walked the beat in Edinburgh Old Town; a bustling part of the city where robbery, drunkenness and disorder were constant. During the long, cold nights, Bobby was Gray's companion. In documents Skye terrier Bobby is described as 'tenacious in character, distrustful of strangers but devoted to family and friends, he was courageous but not aggressive. No other sort of dog has more gritty tenacity, cockiness or sparkle than a Skye terrier with one particular noted quality – loyalty.' After Gray died of tuberculosis in 1858, Bobby's loyalty became a national sensation. Legend has it that the day after Gray's funeral, Bobby was discovered sitting on top of his freshly dug grave in Kirkyard Cemetery. He was ushered away but returned again and again and finally kept a mournful vigil on his master's grave for 14 years until he died in 1872. Given the bond between dog and owner, I've no doubt Bobby was reunited with his owner when he died.

I've often been visited by animal spirits during readings and when I see them it always surprises me for some reason, and it makes me smile. They still retain their playfulness, especially dogs. They can be disruptive in some cases and blunder in just like they do in life.

I was on stage once giving a reading to a girl in the audience. She had lost her friend who had died of leukaemia and she had spent hours with him in hospital as he underwent treatment that sadly proved ineffective. He had come through to say how grateful he was for her support and love and to let her know that although he was terribly ill and weak when he died, he no longer suffered and watched over her from the afterlife. It was a poignant and emotional reading as you can probably imagine.

And then I heard the noise of rubber on wood. I looked down to where the noise was coming from I saw a ball bounce across the stage. A second later a dog ran after it from the left to the right of the stage. It was oblivious to anything else other than the ball. I made a little gasp and stepped back. For a second I couldn't register whether it was a real dog or a dog in spirit. But what would a real dog be doing running across the stage of a psychic show?

I continued with the reading and then I heard it again.

The ball bounced past me once more. To my left I heard panting and the patter of little claws on the wood of the stage. The dog materialised again. It was a small wire-haired terrier with a scruffy tan coat and grey-flecked dark hair hanging like a beard around its muzzle.

It skittered past me and then stopped, turned and trotted back looking up at me. I stared down at it in silence. The audience must have wondered what on earth was going on. Then the cheeky little scamp grabbed the hem of my long coat it is mouth and gave it a tug. Then it trotted off.

As the dog yanked my clothes I shrieked and when I did, so did a woman in the front row of the audience.

I looked at her in amazement.

'You didn't just see what I saw did you?' I asked.

'Something just pulled your coat,' she said. Although she hadn't seen the dog, she had seen my clothes move.

Just as in life, animals can lighten the mood and bring joy and fun. In the middle of one traumatic reading where I was imparting the horrific details of a girl's murder to her friends, a cat suddenly popped up next to me. It had a particularly random name.

'There's no one called Tuppence is there?' I shrugged.

The woman I was speaking to looked even more shocked than she had been before.

'My mum's cat passed, she was called Tuppence.'

'The girl is with Tuppence,' I told her.

What a lovely thought to know that all that love and care we place in our pets serves their energy after they die and allows them to come back and comfort and amuse us when we most need it.

Why is there evil in the world?

It is a question I ask myself all the time because of some the things that I see in my mind's eye. The murders and violence and the nasty things that people do to each other are hard to comprehend and it makes me wonder how it is allowed if there is a divine energy watching over us all. But the answer I believe is that all the evil stays on Earth and is here as a balance. It is not a nice balance but in life there always has to be a balance of things; light and dark, hot and cold, good and bad. I don't know why that is but it seems to be one of the laws of life and nature.

We have to be careful what we mean when we talk about evil as it is a word that is often taken out of context. We use it to describe things that aren't really evil. Some people may be described as evil for an act they have carried out but we don't always know the circumstances which led them to conduct that action. Not every crime or killing is because of an evil act. There can be mitigating circumstances and although it is still wrong to commit crimes, it is not accurate to label them all as evil.

Thankfully pure evil is rare and it is there to be won over. It controls an individual, it manifests itself in a person and it is a force. It is something I have come across twice in my life, which is twice too much as far as I am concerned. Once it came in the form of a man who arrived at my house when I did private readings. He was dressed from head to toe in black and he rode a black motorcycle. I could feel evil on him, seeping from every pore. He was infected with bad energy and it was eating him like cancer. He knew I knew he was evil and as I opened the door to him I was met with a torrent of abuse.

The evil energy reached through him and grabbed me. Awful images of his past flashed into my head. I knew he had been in the Marines and that he had done despicable things. I saw him trying to strangle a young woman on a sofa.

John came to my rescue, grabbed him and bundled him out the door.

I was shaking and in shock. The whole episode lasted less than a minute but it has remained etched on my memory to this day. I discovered later that the man was a former US Marine who had been kicked out of the service because he was obsessed with the occult and was practicing black magic. He tracked me down because he wanted to connect to the afterlife through me. Heaven knows what he wanted to do but I suspect he wasn't after a positive, life-affirming reading.

The other time I was exposed to evil happened when I was a young girl living in Fulham. I have never spoken about it and never will. It happened in the toilet. It wasn't sexual but it was an evil energy. Evil is made of the same fundamental stuff that spiritual energy is but while spiritual energy is positive, evil is negative.

Luckily most people do not come across evil in their lives. You would feel it if you did, even if you were a non-believer. It hangs in the air. People such as priests and witch doctors may experience it because they are asked to expel it when it manifests itself in a person or a place. If a particularly terrible thing has happened somewhere, evil leaves a stain on it. The site of the Twin Towers in New York is an example of this as are the former Nazi concentration camps in Eastern Europe. These sites have a foreboding feel about them.

Sometimes this negative energy attracts spirit, usually it is the victims that return. I believe they return to the sites of their deaths when they didn't get the justice they deserved. They are drawing attention to the injustice as they believe in fairness and that people should account for their actions or repent.

Thankfully good is there to counteract evil. Spirits will come through to help those suffering on Earth plane. They are selfless and they have a sense of justice that burns through brightly when they have been wronged in some way.

At a powerful reading not so long ago, the spirit of a murdered girl came through. Her friends and family were in the audience and immediately took the message. The spirit had been with me all evening. There was urgency about the message she had for her loved ones. She showed me many details of where the crime had taken place. She showed me the copse where her body had been found, she showed me the man who had killed her and also showed me how he had tried to conceal her body using heavy stones. It was horrific and unsettling but she was communicating these details because no trial had taken place. She wanted justice.

'She was here first of all when the show started,' I told the people in the audience.

'She is definitely aware of who did it to her.'

I have also experienced readings where a spirit has come through full of remorse for the terrible acts that they carried out when they were alive. For example at one show several years ago the spirit of a man who murdered a girl came through. He had a message for a girl in the audience who knew the victim. Following the crime he had taken his own life as he was full of guilt. He wanted to apologise for what he had done.

They often come through looking for forgiveness, even when what they did may not seem so bad. Some crimes are viewed less harshly with the passing of time. One spirit who came through appeared distressed. He had a terrible burns injury along his side. I could smell burnt flesh.

'I didn't mean it,' he was repeating. And when I saw an image of him in my mind's eye he looked terribly thin. I sensed he was hungry.

A girl took the message, the names I had provided and the details resonated with her and told the story of a relative she had heard about from her extended family.

The spirit was a boy who lived in Liverpool. He came from a very poor family and was malnourished. They had no money for food and one day, to try and raise funds, the boy had taken one of his friends to a local railway track and tried to steal some of the metal to sell for scrap. He had been electrocuted and died. Although most people would understand and sympathise with the reasons behind the boy's crime, he was still looking for forgiveness.

'He's saying "I didn't mean it". He wanted the money for food,' I told the girl.

It's debatable whether this boy was bad, let alone evil. I believe pure evil does not have the capacity to repent. I also believe that if you die at the hands of evil you are elevated to a higher level. You get a fast track ticket to divinity. If you are evil, when you die that evil force within you stays here. When you trust in spirit world, you also trust in the fact that there is evil and that it exists here on Earth.

We are not born evil, it is a force that manifests itself in us in life and we have more chance of attracting that evil energy if we are open to it in the same way we are more susceptible to good spiritual energy if we are open to it. So be good and love life!

Can you predict the lottery?

No. I've tried, and that's the truth! I've sat in front of the television when the draw is about to be made and opened myself to spirit. My mind goes blank. It doesn't work.

In Australia I did shows in a number of Returned and Services League Clubs, which are similar to our British Legion Clubs but on a much, much bigger scale. They have bars, restaurants, casinos and auditoriums in them. Many of them have lines of slot machines in them. The Aussies call them Pokies. Our roadie on the tour tried to persuade me to play, perhaps he was hoping my psychic ability would help me hit the jackpot but just as I knew I couldn't predict a win I also knew I wouldn't win anything, which was probably more about my common sense than my gift.

Perhaps I'm not allowed to pick the lottery numbers so I continue to do the work I do. If I could chose the winning numbers week in and week out I would be on a yacht in the South of France next to Simon Cowell by now, not at a theatre in the East Midlands (not that I have anything against the East Midlands, it's a lovely place – it's just that the South of France is warmer).

There has only ever been once that I have been

allowed to use my gift to win something and that was for a woman who came to see me when I practiced at home. She had been a good person all her life, had devoted herself to caring for people and that devotion had led her to become very poor. She'd given up work to care for sick family members and was in a lot of financial difficulty. During the reading I was given a series of numbers at different intervals. They made no sense to her at the time but she wrote them down. There were six numbers in all.

After the reading she felt the impulse to buy a lottery ticket and used the random numbers I had given her. She won £90,000! With the money she was able to buy her council house. After the win she invited me to the celebration party she threw and there were 200 people there. Everyone there wanted the winning numbers for that weekend. I had to tell them it was a fluke; a one off. The lady had been so hard up spirit gave her the numbers to reward her for the sacrifices she had made. She was a good, kind person. Oddly I did not buy a ticket myself that week. I felt inside that if I did I would have been breaking a rule. Instinctively I knew it would not be right.

Money means nothing to spirit. The old saying "you can't take it with you when you go" is right. By all means be sensible with money and if you can, make sure you can look after your children or loved ones when you go but enjoy it while you can. Love is the currency in the afterlife so you should stock up on that while you are alive instead.

Spirits don't like greed. They have opinions about it that they are all too keen to offer to the living sometimes.

At a show in Scotland a small man called Alec came through. He was showing me a house with two white columns outside. He was dressed in clothes that were too big for him and although his demeanour could be best described as grumpy, I got the impression that he was just a man of few words and a bit of a loner. He gave me the name James and Jeanie.

A lady in the audience put her hand up and explained that she believed it was a man who lived in a house near her. His soul was in the house.

'He haunts the house,' I told her.

'He's got the hump, someone got the money when the house got sold,' I said.

'That'll be Thomas, one of his relatives,' she said.

Alec was also concerned that when he died the house was cleared and a lot of his possessions were sold off cheaply or given away for nothing. He thought that it was unfair that many of the things he had worked hard to buy in his life had been passed over so cheaply. He wasn't bothered about the monetary value; the items were useless to him where he was! He was more concerned about the fairness of the situation and the respect that he felt should have been shown to him and the trappings of his life. In life he believed the things he surrounded himself with formed part of his personality and that it was disrespectful to have disposed of them without thought.

While spirits are unlikely to provide you with the means to get rich quick, your own intuition could be the key to improving your lot in life. While I don't believe in luck per se, I do believe that people who have a positive disposition will attract possibilities and are more likely to take them. We create our own luck in life you see and sometimes if we get a hunch about something, it's worth playing that hunch.

For example if you never do the lottery but one day have the urge to buy a ticket, follow your instincts. For £1 you'd be mad not too. It is all about trusting. In life if you get the urge to do something you don't usually do, you should trust your gut. If you dream about a name and notice a horse running the next day with the same name, put a bet on it. You might be pleasantly surprised by the result.

What is déjà vu and premonition?
Can spirits come to us in our dreams?

How many times have you been in a situation and suddenly got the overpowering feeling that you have been there before? We all have. That's déjà vu and it's one of the weirdest sensations we get (I'm discounting the feeling of being contacted by the dead here as that's not something that happens to most people). So what is déjà vu? What causes it? I believe it's something to do with time and spirit. Remember I said earlier that the realm of spirit isn't governed by the same laws of space and time that our world is? Well perhaps déjà vu is when we connect to that world or when that world brushes against ours and funny things happen to our perception of time. Maybe momentarily we live the same moment twice and that is what causes the strange feeling of familiarity.

Déjà vu is different to premonition, which is a strong sense that something is about to happen. Throughout history there have been many people who have had premonitions about tragedies and historical events. For example in 1966 a junior school in Aberfan, Wales was engulfed in a killer landslide. 116 children died in the disaster including ten-year-old Eryl Mai Jones. In the days leading up to the landslide she had told her mother about disturbing dreams she was having. She described how she dreamt her school had disappeared after "something black had come down over it". Eryl Mai had a premonition of her own death.

It seems that the bigger the event, the more reports there are afterwards of people who had foreseen it. Before the Titanic's fateful maiden voyage many passengers reported a sense of foreboding and J. P. Morgan, the famous US financier who was one of the richest men in the world at the time and who had links to the company which owned the ship, cancelled his ticket at the last minute.

Many stories surfaced in the months after the terrorist attacks on the Twin Towers. One woman reported a dream in which she experienced spinning into blackness and heard voices repeating the number 2,830. She also heard a name which sounded like "Horooks". She was so disturbed by the dream that she cancelled air tickets she had booked for September 11.

It transpired that 2,830 was the number of reported deaths at the time of the attack and the first officer of Flight 175 which crashed into the South Tower was Michael Horrocks.

Scientists have studied premonitions and some have theories about what could cause them. One doctor, Larry Dossey, wrote a book about them, *The Power Of Premonitions: How Knowing The Future Can Shape Our Lives*. His explanation is that premonition is a natural sense we have developed to warn us of impending danger. He believes we are more likely to have premonitions about those to whom we are emotionally attached because we have strong subconscious links to them. This theory may be right as neurologists have studied the links between some particularly close individuals, such as twins and have discovered some strange examples where people register feeling uneasy at times when their loved ones are in danger or are ill. Could this be what telepathy is?

I believe there is a psychic aspect to premonition, which could also be described as clairvoyance. It is actually part of our natural form of intuitiveness and it can be developed. You can make yourself more open to premonition. It is part of the spectrum of psychic ability and it starts by trusting in those dreams and instincts and listening to what they are telling you. The more you trust the more you will move along that spectrum. Before our lives became modern in the technological sense of the word, before we relied on machines, computers and industry to look after us, we lived much closer to the land and to nature and instead relied on our instincts for survival. Those instincts would have seemed much like premonition and they have been blunted over time.

There is a spiritual element to premonition too. And this is apparent in the fact that many people report that they have premonitions through dreams. These are not dreams at all. They are your loved ones in spirit visiting you and warning you. They can foresee things because time isn't the same in their world. The future, past and present all mesh into one. A dream can be a premonition or it can be a sign. When you dream about a departed loved one, they are there with you. Dreams are the most common way they come through because when you are asleep and that conscious part of your mind is shut down, your guard is down. There are no distractions; no television, no noise, no people. It is easier for them to enter your mind. The pathway in is clear. It can be one of the most effective ways spirits can contact people who are not listening and who are not open to signs.

Spirits will look for these times when you are switched off and relaxed to connect and if you want to invite them in you should try and relax more. All of us have our own ways of relaxation when we lead fast lives and it is at those moments when our minds are still. For me, it's when I have a wee in the morning. I sit there half asleep and just enjoy the quiet and peace of the moment. If anyone was going to come through, it would be then, on the toilet! I also tickle my left shoulder each morning and that calms me. I have never meditated so I am not an advocate but for others that process of entering a state of relaxation and calming the mind down could definitely be beneficial to spiritual awakening and psychic links.

I don't believe in the afterlife.
How do I overcome doubt?

There will always be people who think that once you are dead that is it, the end! There will always be people who think we do not have souls and that we do not possess psychic energy. There will always be doubt. You might be surprised to know that I welcome that. I think it is a good thing. We are meant to doubt. Doubt makes us ask questions and because of that it gives us answers. It is as important as knowing. Since I have had the opportunity to perform live readings at theatre shows my psychic ability has been stretched in new ways and people asked questions of me which in turn made me question what happens when large numbers of people come together for psychic readings I learned more and I understood more. Doubt is very good for you; it's the mental equivalent of pumping iron.

But just because you have doubts about something, doesn't mean it does not exist. Doubt doesn't mean you should discount something altogether just because you don't understand it. This is where the sceptics get it wrong. They dismiss out of hand. We can't see sub-atomic particles and atoms but we know they are there. At the end of the day, when it comes to psychic events and messages from the dead, something is happening and I am proof of that. But because addressing that means going against vocal sections of society which refuse to acknowledge the afterlife, the sceptics will refuse to look at the issue objectively. They have their own agenda.

Many of the people who come to my shows have doubts and I am privileged that I can answer them with solid validation. For example at one show the messages were zinging in thick and fast. I was trying my best to juggle them. One was leading on from the other like a psychic trail stretching in to the night. I kept seeing a St Christopher on a gold chain. I couldn't quite work out which message it related to and where it fitted in with the evening because there were so many that were interlinked that night.

Finally a lady stood to take it.

'I put a St Christopher on this evening because I was hoping my dad might come through. I have never worn it before,' she said. She was doubtful the pendant would work, but she was open to the possibility that maybe her father would show himself.

A name popped into my.

'Was your father called Gordon?' I asked.

'No... that was his brother. He's in spirit.'

'And is there the name Duncan?'

'That was his other brother,' she confirmed. 'I didn't believe this before I came.' She was nothing if not honest.

I told her that it was ok to have doubts. I still do

because sometimes what happens to me seems so mad.

'I still struggle with knowing what I do,' I told her. 'Yet it happens. All I know is I see, touch, smell and taste spirit and I get things in my head.'

Even if you have doubts I would urge you to open yourself up to possibility just as that lady did. You don't have to have a specific belief set, you just need to trust in the love you have for your departed loved ones. During my stage shows I ask the audience to bring along photographs of their loved ones and write letters to people in spirit they want to contact. Just that simple act of remembrance makes a connection. For example a woman at a recent show left a letter and a photograph. Randomly I pulled the letter out, and then later in the show I pulled out her photograph. There are hundreds of cards and photos left each night so the odds that I would pick two from the same person on the same night were huge. Yet it happened and it happened because the spirit that the lady wanted so desperately to contact directed it. It was not a random coincidence.

The spirit was her son. He had died in an accident. He gave me many signs to validate the reading. He told me he had wanted to go to Australia. His mother confirmed he had told her this a few days before he died in an accident. I saw the scene after the accident, he had massive head injuries.

The lady explained that she had spoken to him earlier that day and asked him to do his best to come through. He had. His energy was so strong that other spirits used it to come through that night.

Suddenly, as I was reading for the lady, a small dog appeared in my mind. I knew his name was Teddy. I asked the lady if she owned a dog called Teddy. The audience laughed. It was such a random question and went some way to diffuse the emotional reading. She was bemused and shook her head. Then a lady sitting next to her, who she did not know, admitted that Teddy was her dog.

It was the first time I had done a card and photograph at the same venue for the same person. It was a real 'wow!' moment.

It is usually men who doubt. At a show in Australia a man was with his wife in the audience and I picked him out because there was a spirit coming through to me who wanted to give him a message. He was a big man, a proper Aussie bloke, and he raised a quizzical eyebrow when I pointed him out. He was totally sceptical. His father was in spirit and I got his name, then his father told me the nickname he was called when he was younger. I could see the doubt peel away from this man as he stood and listened to the details I was giving him. He started to well up.

After the show he came up to me as I was signing books and he was a changed man. He explained that he had arrived that evening as a sceptic but was leaving with belief and that he had undergone a life-changing experience. While it is flattering to think that what I do could have a profound effect on people, it is not down to me to change anyone's beliefs. I don't have a purpose or an agenda. I just say what spirit tells me to say.

In life, if you are prepared to open your mind up to the possibility you will be amazed what you will find. If what I do allows people who have doubts to be open to the possibility that there is an after-life, then that can only be a good thing. And it is my belief that one day we will be able to start to understand what really happens to us after we die in a fully comprehensive way.

Even sceptics can be persuaded and it's never too late to overcome their cynicism. I have had hundreds of sceptics who come through to me from the afterlife. On one memorable occasion a man's three daughters were in the audience. He was a total non-believer throughout his life time but he came through with his message loud and clear and there was a huge amount of energy radiating from him as he connected with his children. They told me all through his life, whenever he heard about mediums, he would scoff and discount them as a load of rubbish. Nevertheless when it came to the opportunity, he was the first to come through and make contact, even though there were other relatives of the girls in spirit waiting to come through. He barged his way to the front of the queue! I smile when I think what a very pleasant surprise it would have been for him when he passed and realised death was just the beginning.

Why are spirits with us, what is their purpose? Can they help me?

Quite simply they are here because we will them to come and their purpose is love. They can help us and guide us and they do that out of unconditional love. They are here to maintain the link in the chain between our world and their world.

They can help us in many ways. They can warn us of dangers either through signs, in dreams or, in the most wonderful instances through direct contact. On the surface level they are there to help us with our grief. It is amazing to see how they come through to grieving relatives and give them validation of an afterlife. I've given so many readings were a spirit has appeared and given the receiver such specific information that there is no doubt left. As we get older spirit is also there to help us come to terms with our own mortality and to give us reassurance that life does go on. They are there at the very end of our lives to help us when we pass and to guide us. They are there to let the world know what a glorious place the afterlife is. They do not come reluctantly. If you open yourself to them they will be there. They don't need much encouragement. I do not call the dead, I do not wake anyone from slumber, they come to me and that's the natural order of things.

While the overriding reasons they come are love and validation, some come through with a purpose more defined. I know what an incredible privilege it is to be able to pass on a message. I am allowed to do what I do because the spirits will it and so when they give me information I know that I must pass it on without revision and as it is told to me. They use the link I have with them for a number of reasons. Often they just want to say 'hello' and give a cheery wave from the afterlife but there are other reasons. Sometimes they want to apologise for things they did in life and sometimes they want to heal family rifts. When they do I can feel like a psychic Jeremy Kyle!

I was recently at a show in Hampshire. The words were faint at first. "Pad. Pad." Initially I thought I was being given a name, Paddy or Pat. But as I became more attuned the fog cleared and I could feel him. There was a sense of suddenly being picked up and carried, and then the name Andrew.

'Don't change his name,' he was saying.

There was a sense of urgency to this message and the spirit delivering it had already tried to show himself to the intended receiver.

A woman put her hand up to take the message.

'I know a soldier who was blown up in Afghan. He stood on a pad which set off a bomb. His name was Andrew.'

It transpired that Andrew had a son and an ex wife and that there were suspicions that the former spouse was thinking of changing the son's name. Andrew had come through to register his opposition to her plans.

'He's got my name,' the spirit said. And after that he went.

At a show in Scotland, a spirit came through with the name Derek. He was full of apology. He wanted to say sorry for the state he left when he died. I got the names Elaine and Helen. A lady called Elaine stood up. Derek was her cousin. She explained that the circumstances leading up to his death were traumatic and that she was there throughout. Derek wanted to make things right. Just before I gave the message, which I had no doubt was for the lady who took it, a man in the audience had raised his hand when he heard me say the name Helen and as he did and I caught his eye I felt a jolt from spirit. I knew there was someone in spirit with a connection to him so as soon as Derek had left me I went to him.

He explained that his grandmother was Helen. I had her in spirit along with a little baby boy and his grandfather. I suspected he had been born prematurely. I told the man this and he confirmed that he had lost a baby son. I reassured him that the child was with his ancestors and was at peace. Then I got the name Andy and the sense that there was much tension between this man in the audience and Andy.

'You will be gentle with Andy,' I said, 'don't get angry with him. He has good feelings for you. Are you estranged from him?'

The man confirmed that Andy was his father. When his son had been born it had caused a massive rift in the family and he no longer spoke to his dad. His grandfather who was with the boy in spirit was explaining that the rift should be healed. It had also affected his relationship with his mother who he no longer spoke to either. The family had been torn apart by these events and the family members in spirit wanted everybody to bury the hatchet and make up.

'This baby's loss polarised the family,' I said. 'This man who has your baby in his arms and loves him is saying don't be hard on Andy, give him a bit of slack.'

The grandfather also gave me the name Charlie. The man in the audience explained that his grandfather's brother was Charles. I saw a scene. There was a locked door and a desperate attempt to get through it. The man explained that when his grandmother had died his grandfather had locked the front door and that to get to her he had to go round the back of the house to get in.

'They all love you,' I told him. 'They are showing you what a good boy you are.' The overriding sense I had was that these spirits from the man's family were trying to get their living relatives to forgive and forget.

'Your mum is just trying her best to live her life,' I told him. 'You are part of your mum and Andy is part of her life and for whatever reason she stays with him. You have to be in touch with your mother, this is without a doubt. This is an incredible message for you and you are very generous for allowing us to be part of that.'

It was a very special message and an illustration of how spirit comes back to help and guide us.

How do I choose a good medium?

Thankfully there are good mediums out there doing very good and worthwhile work but unfortunately there are more bad mediums than good ones and also many complete charlatans who are just out to take your money. While we all have to make a living and pay the bills I do believe that if you are going to charge for a service, you should deliver that service. Proper mediums will have their own set of ethics and should be able to tell you about themselves and their work and why they are qualified to give readings before you book to see them. You should question their motives. Good mediums have a sense of purpose in their work.

So how do you know which mediums are good? First and foremost is word of mouth and recommendation. Where you can, get a referral from someone you know and trust. You might not think you know anyone who has been to see a medium but I bet you do. Thousands of people visit them every year. If you know someone who has been and who had a positive experience it is better than choosing one at random from the internet. If you are still wary ask the psychic for testimonials. Many modern psychics have websites and they often give a flavour of the type of business and reading the medium conducts. If someone has a website that looks professional and looks professionally designed, rather than thrown together, that usually suggests they have invested in their business and so are serious about it.

It is also worth taking into account how long a psychic has been practising professionally. If someone has been a full time psychic for 20 or 30 years, the chances are they have been successful and are consequently decent and genuine.

Rather than relying on Google, I would recommend getting in contact with your nearest spiritualist church and asking them. It doesn't matter if you are religious or believe in Spiritualism as a religion, they should be able to help as there will be people within the church who work as mediums and do private sittings.

Another reputable avenue to look down is The College of Psychic Studies which is based in London and was founded 125 years ago by a group of eminent scholars and scientists. Its purpose was to facilitate formal investigation into the psychic and mediumistic phenomena that were such a topic of debate in the Victoria era. They have a lot of good mediums there.

Before you even start looking for a medium I would suggest that you think about the reasons you want to visit one. There are usually two; curiosity and the desire to contact someone specific in spirit. Both are valid reasons and a bad experience can damage any future urges you may have to see other mediums. At its worst a bad experience can leave the client with doubt that the afterlife exists at all. If this happens to you please remember it is not spirit world that is the problem, it is the medium. If your reasons are mercenary and self serving, if you want to know whether you will be famous or how to get rich, you will never be satisfied because you will not get the answers you want to hear from a decent psychic.

Once you have found someone you feel is right, whether through recommendation or research, call them and speak to them first. Get a feel for them. Do they seem friendly and kind? Do you feel you can trust them? Use your instincts and your intuition.

I have had many rewarding and long-term relationships with people I have seen over many years and a single reading can develop into a lifelong relationship. There needs to be trust between the two of you, as it is a two-way relationship. The better you and your medium click, the more enriching you will find the reading.

There are certain factors that make someone a good medium. A good medium needs to have lived a little and to have had life experiences. Mediums need empathy and most of us develop empathy through our lives. I'm not saying you can't be young and be a medium but you need someone who knows how to explain what is happening during the reading clearly and sympathetically. Personally I know I could not have done what I do today when I was in my twenties. It has taken me many decades to develop my gift to the level it is today.

Finally, the best way to judge a medium is through their accuracy. That is the benchmark. How accurate are they? How many hits do they get? It does help to be a nice person, but without accuracy you will not succeed as a professional medium. You need a bedside manner but it is not good if you are getting things wrong.

I have phonelines for fans to call for readings which are manned by mediums that have been vetted to make sure they reach good standards of mediumship.

In honesty it is hard to find a good medium with all the attributes – accuracy, kindness, approach-ability, sense of humour, experience, empathy. There is a community and it is a competitive business. In truth I tend to keep myself to myself and let my accuracy speak for itself. There are always mediums out there to suit any pockets and the most expensive is not always the best.

When is it right to let someone go, what are the stages?

We are never and should never forget our dead but there are times when maybe we can move on after they have gone. It really does depend on the individual. For some the process takes many years.

Initially, when grief is raw, the stages are shock, bewilderment, confusion and denial. There can be anger and guilt too which are very much mixed together at the beginning. They go hand in hand, you are angry that you didn't do enough and guilty too. Then there can be a period of complete calm, almost euphoria. It is as if, to protect yourself from the feelings that are overpowering you, your body floods itself with adrenaline and stops you feeling.

As you continue through the grief process you may begin to learn to cope without that person but there will always be reminders. There will be certain places, smells, sights, sounds, songs and even people that will trigger a memory or a thought, usually totally out of the blue, and the emotional freefall begins over again. It presents itself in many ways; crying, not eating, becoming withdrawn.

Grief never stops. You just find a way you are able to put that grief into an area of your brain where you can cope with it.

Later, the process of moving on begins. It starts

with practical actions such as removing your loved one's name from your bills or your joint accounts, or erasing their voice from the answer phone machine. This stage is fraught with guilt. You feel like you are letting that person down. Do not worry. It is hard and they do understand.

If there are items that you feel you need to remove, such as photographs that are too painful to look at, store them in a memory box. When you feel stronger and more able to concentrate on the good, happy memories you will have you can look at them. No one should ever be forced to get rid of personal belongings and things that were precious to the person who has died. Bereaved people need to be able to take their time. I feel sad when I hear about people who have bagged up someone's belongings soon after they died and taken them all to the charity shop or put them all on eBay. I guarantee that in those circumstances a few weeks or months down the road there will be regret. If you feel the need to remove belongings, perhaps ask another member of family if they would like them instead of throwing them out completely.

Once a young girl came to see me. She was lovely, her aunt had died and she had loved her very much. Her mother had passed her aunt's bracelet to her. Three or four years later she came to me and said every time she wore it her mum cried and wanted the bracelet back. The daughter didn't want to give it back.

'When did your mum give it to you?' I asked.

'The day after my aunt died,' she replied.

I had to be honest with her.

'Your mum was not thinking straight. She was devastated and she could see you were devastated too and wanted to ease your pain away so she gave you the bracelet. She was only doing it out of love. Now she can see you are coping with your aunt's death she is looking at her own grief and that bracelet is a link to her sister.'

It was a fair assessment. I do not know whether they sorted out their differences but it illustrates how carefully people need to consider what to do with possessions after a death in the family. I would say don't throw anything away immediately. Wait. In fact I find the idea of getting rid of things heartbreaking.

Spirits tend to agree. They like us to hold onto sentimental items because they act as links to Earth plane.

A girl came through during a reading in Scotland. Her name was Nicole and she had left a baby on Earth plane.

'Don't throw my picture away,' she was telling me.

The message was for a lady in the audience who became emotional as the details emerged. When I mentioned the picture she began to cry.

'Take it out of the bin,' the girl was saying.

'You haven't put her picture in the bin have you love?' I asked.

She held the microphone and explained: 'I did

last year before anything happened to her and I thought I wouldn't need them.'

At the same reading another message came through with a similar theme – again, the power of message building was in full flow. The lady in spirit was Mary. She was showing me art work and pictures hanging on a wall. She also showed me a mass of grey hair neatly tied in a bun. I had a feeling that the hair had been cut and explained this to the audience.

A lady stood to take the message.

'My mother was Mary, she was very artistic. She did embroidery; I have them framed around the house. She also had grey hair tied in a bun.'

'Did you cut her hair off? She's showing me someone holding hair with a green ribbon around it,' I asked.

'I didn't cut her hair but I can tell you what that is.'

She went on to explain that as a girl she had hair so long it stretched down her back. When she was 15 she went to the hairdressers to have it all cut off. There was so much of it that the hairdresser offered to buy it to make hairpieces from it. But Mary refused, took it home and tied it with a green ribbon.

'I have it in a bag at the top of my wardrobe. I've kept it all this time,' she finished.

The audience applauded.

'Your mummy can see that darling,' I told her. 'You must never get rid of that. That's her baby's hair.'

We can't keep hold of every photo and memento we collect through life but there is a meaning to each and every one of them. It is healthy in time to let go of the physical things we possess that remind us of our departed loved ones but the important things should be cherished.

It is not always good for bereaved people to continue surrounding themselves with mementos as they can sometimes stop us from moving forward. However, think carefully before you throw stuff away. An image can sometimes be a captured soul. There is a tribe in Africa which is reluctant to have their photographs taken because they feel that each photo takes a little bit of their soul away. I'm not saying we do that when we take pictures of loved ones but ever since I was a little girl I've realised that photos hold energy. Every image is a moment in time and should be cherished.

There are other ways to keep memories. When we have children we should pass down anecdotes and stories that were passed down to us about our family. My grandfather, George, used to tell me about how he sold strawberries outside Southfields station in South West London. He used to mimic the market stall banter and told me about all the scrapes he got into. I would crack up. I told the same stories to my children when they were little and they now tell it to their children. It keeps Granddad George alive.

In time perhaps, when all links to Earth plane are gone, maybe that's when spirits finally let go and are able to move on to divinity; when they have nothing to come back for. However, even for people with no direct relatives alive and no more possessions on Earth plane, there will always be some distant link. As we do more research and get more interested in genealogy people make more links to their past. Memories are easier to keep alive thanks to the digital age. Family trees show that every one of us has links, even if we never marry or have kids we are still linked to others. Even if people die and are never spoken of, it doesn't mean that the echo they leave on the earth is not there.

The way we remember our loved ones is incredibly personal. What we decide to keep is an individual choice. I have a friend whose husband died young. He was in his thirties and he fell off some scaffolding. Years later she met a new man and moved in with him. They were very happy. She had all her former husband's clothes in boxes in the garage and one day the guy she was living with asked me for some advice. Should she get rid of them? I explained that it shouldn't bother him. She said that every now and then she felt him around her and walking in the garage kept him alive in her head. She kept it all.

For people who lose a spouse or a partner, the final piece of letting go can be when they decide to have another relationship. Again this decision will be full of questions and doubts and again the decision is up to the individual. There are no hard and fast rules. Some people move on quickly because they are afraid of being alone. They panic. Some people find themselves helpless when they are alone and want someone to be there for practical reasons, not for emotional reasons. Our loved ones are in such a wonderful place they want us to be in a wonderful place down here and if that means that we are able to love another person they are happy for us. You will love that other person differently. If that person is meant to be in our lives they will love us and understand the complexity of the situation. I've never come across a spirit who was angry that someone had moved on. Sometimes they have a laugh. They look out for people.

How do I cope with terminal illness?

You can grieve for someone before they die when they are terminally ill and you know they are going to die. That is when the grief process begins. Or when they have suffered catastrophic injury or illness and are brain dead in a coma with no hope of recovery.

In this terrible situation most sensible people assume they would start to prepare themselves on a practical level by getting things like wills and life insurance policies sorted out. However, in my experience I have found that many people can't bring themselves to do this because to actually move forward in your head and accept that life is coming to an end is very hard. All those involved need support from others to cope with the fact that time is running out. A lot of people will go into denial. The person dying often goes into a state of denial because they can't accept the prognosis and even if they do, they do not want to upset their loved ones. And loved ones worry that by accepting fate they are in some unconscious way almost wishing someone dead.

The only way of approaching terminal illness is with honesty, even if that means telling that person what they don't want to hear. They often do not want to hear the truth so it is your job as a true friend to help them understand the situation. Talk to them compassionately and honestly and be strong.

It is important, no matter how hard it may be, to tell your adult loved ones and friends about the situation. If, for example, you have been told that your husband is terminally ill and you choose not tell your grown up children because you do not want to upset them, they will not thank you because they need to know so they can make their own arrangements. Tough love plays a part. A lot of people skirt around the issue but it needs to be addressed.

It is even a good idea to write down your plans; your goodbye plan. Let your loved ones know what your wishes are. On a practical level make a will and make sure your affairs are all in order so you do not have to worry about the little things as the illness progresses.

Let those around you who will be left know what your wishes are, from the music and theme of your funeral to your wishes regarding treatment should you become too ill to make your own choices. Do you want to be kept alive on a life support machine? This is a big question because families struggle to know what to do for the best. Personally I believe that when a patient is brain dead they are closer to spirit than to the living world. You need to listen to the medical profession when they tell you someone is in a vegetative state and they will never wake. There have been occasions where people have woken but they have never been the same. I get lots of messages at shows where the person in spirit has been in a coma and relatives have switched off the machine and the person in spirits always thanks them. Others come through who have been kept alive in a vegetative state and explain how awful it was.

I have often been told by spirits who died after being resuscitated, sometimes several times, how they were pulled back and forth between Earth plane and the afterlife. They describe it as being in limbo.

As you put affairs in order also put relationships in order. It is harder to make up with people and say sorry when you are divided by death so sort out the emotional things that need sorting out. You may have been feuding with family members for years but nothing is ever as bad as it seems. If there is something you always wanted to say, negative or positive, say it. Clear the air. Don't be self-indulgent and just off-load, but while there is time to have a conversation, do it.

Tell people who need to be told how much you love them.

Dealing with a child who is terminally ill must be one of the hardest things in the world to face. I have nothing but admiration for people who find themselves in this terrible position and I would recommend that anyone who does finds help and support through the services available. Charities such as Make A Wish Foundation and Starlight can help and your GP should be able to recommend good counselling services. I think it is important to remain positive around the child and to make the most of the days you have without dwelling on the situation.

If you are speaking to someone you know who is terminally ill, invoke all the good memories. Sit with them and recount the good times you lived through. Try not to be morbid. Passing for people who are terminally ill is often a release.

Can I be a medium?

First the good news. We all have the latent ability to experience spirit world, that means everyone of us can feel our loved ones in the afterlife and connect with them on some level. Now the bad news. Just because we are all psychic doesn't mean we can all be psychics – which is the more commonly used phrase for a medium. The main ingredient required to develop a psychic ability beyond the basics we all have is trust. You have to listen to the signs and trust in them. It sounds easy doesn't it? It is not, and the main reason for that is because other people become barriers. As soon as you start telling people you are flexing your psychic muscle they will try and dissuade you. They will squash it in the same way that parents inadvertently squash the psychic ability of their sons and daughters. For this reason, at first, it is best to keep things to yourself or just tell those you trust and who share similar views. For example you may wake in the morning of the anniversary of your mother's death and see a robin sitting on your windowsill. That is a sign. That is your mum nudging you. Believe it and acknowledge it. But if you tell someone who is cynical they will put it down to coincidence and possibly laugh. That might dissuade you. So keep it to yourself, recognise what it means and say a little thank you to your mum for the sign. If spirit knows you are open they will call again and the next time the sign will be stronger.

If you dismiss it, you lose it. You need to exercise it and the more you exercise it, the stronger it becomes. They are your relatives and loved ones, they want to come and speak to you. The trust you place in the signs they send is a torch. It is a light of hope you can shine on someone for a moment.

We think of them and they are there. Our thoughts are an umbilical cord of love. Sometimes, in grief, it feels as though that is not good enough. We can never bring them back. But trust in the afterlife and the signs it shows us is a torchlight that illuminates the dark corners and shines a light on them and their memories.

Becoming more psychic is a gradual thing. It doesn't happen overnight. Be consistent and genuine.

Your level of ability will depend on how you interact with spirit. I believe that my early life was a testing phase to see if I could cope with my gift or if I would scream and run away. I was shown things from a very early age and instead of getting scared and freaking out or denying what I was feeling, I was accepting and inquisitive. I was also lucky enough to have a mother who accepted my ability and didn't discourage it. The spirits saw this and knew that I was a good candidate. They also knew I would develop the sort of personality which would make me a good medium because it's not just about the gift. You also need to have the personality to deliver messages effectively. You need to be a good people person, have a sense of humour and be likeable and approachable. No one wants to see a miserable medium and if no one wants to see you there is not much point having a gift!

To be psychic you need to be as natural and true to yourself as possible. You have to have passion for your work and realise that it is not always about speed, it can be about listening.

As psychics develop they get shown more and more. Sometimes what they see is not pleasant. Spirit may decide to give a warning through a message. A good psychic will use judgement and deliver this in a palatable way so as not to scare the receiver. There are ways to give bad news and if you cannot come up with good ways, sometimes it is best to say nothing. If you cannot think of ways to say anything loving then you are not meant to be a medium.

For example I have a certain style. I am a medium who works in an entertaining way. That is not everyone's cup of tea because I am working with subject matter that shouldn't be entertaining. But I am what I am and I would not change that. In fact I believe if I changed the way I acted I would no longer be able to practice at the high level I do. Again I think I was singled out to do my work by a higher power because of the way I deliver messages. I may be unconventional but I am getting people to consider loss and death who wouldn't normally think about them; and that is a good thing.

There is a bewildering array of courses for people who want to become more psychic. There are residential courses, distance learning courses, online courses. I've never felt the need to do one so I'm not best qualified to judge whether they are beneficial or not. At the end of the day you will never know until you try them. If they are delivered with good intentions they may help but I'm not sure they will make people into effective mediums because the skills you need come from within and are not easily taught in a classroom.

Will spirits warn me if I'm about to have a heart attack?

Our dearly departed don't let death change the fact that they care deeply for us and from their elevated vantage point in the afterlife they can see more than we can. They can see what life has in store for us and they can see whether there are problems on the horizon. They can see if we are due health problems.

I am speaking from firsthand experience. Not only are health and health problems one of the recurring themes during my shows, I was warned about an impending personal health disaster by a loved one in spirit several years ago.

I was preparing to go on stage when I started to feel a pain. Not a terrible agonising pain, but a niggling ache in my hips and knees. It had nothing to do with pre-stage nerves. It was to do with size. At the time I was morbidly obese. I was larger-than-life Sally Morgan. Medium extra large. Newspapers had this way of describing me, the same way they describe other overweight celebrities. "Bubbly" they called me, which really meant fat. My weight hovered around 20 stone and the ache was my hip telling me I wasn't getting any thinner.

I was always aware of my size. I wore size 26 to 28 clothes. But it never really bothered me. It was part of who I was; part of what I was. I was happy in myself, I was confident and successful. However, after a year on the road spending up to four nights a week on stage on my feet and more hours than I care to remember cooped up in cars, my hips had really started playing up. Most nights I'd reach the stage wings puffing. I'd have to stand there and catch my breath before lumbering on stage.

On the night in question as I stood in the darkness catching my breath and aching, listening to the video montage playing on the screen on the stage, one thought, one voice kept reverberating around in my mind.

'You can't go on like this Sally, you can't go on like this Sally.'

I remember it so clearly. It was a male voice, stern and authoritative, but also full of love and concern. And I knew straight away who it was. My Grandpa George. He was mum's dad and was a lovely man. He died of cancer and we'd always shared a special bond when he was alive. He was a kind man and funny without realising just how humourous he could be, which made him even more endearing. He lived for his horse racing and loved a punt on the gee-gees. He always had the racing papers and studied form like it was a science.

And that night he was telling me enough was enough. He was warning me that I'd reached the limit of what my body could cope with and that if I didn't do something drastic and quickly, I'd be joining him in spirit. It was like a light coming on in my head. It was my epiphany and it was the moment I realised that I was dying. I was eating myself to death. I also realised that larger-than-life Psychic Sally's days were numbered – literally if I didn't do something about my weight.

The very next day I called a clinic which specialised in weight loss surgery and several months later went under the knife to have a gastric by-pass. If I hadn't had that surgery I would be dead now, that's not the psychic Sally talking, it is common sense. I had already suffered one minor heart attack and I was on the way to another.

Our health issues are earthly matters and spirits come to us and warn us about them because they do not want to see us suffer. I'm not a doctor and never have been so I am not qualified to dish out medical advice, however, often a spirit will flag up a health matter.

An example of this happened in the north of England at a show.

A man called Jim was in spirit and connected to a receiver in the audience. Jim was a tall man and was holding a new born baby which had passed a few days after it had been born. He'd given me a date: September 6th. The message had been validated by the lady who took it. She told me her uncle Jim had been born on that date and that she knew about the baby.

'Do not cancel your X-ray!' I recounted the words as Jim put them in my mind.

The woman gasped.

'You have to have that done. You need that.'

The lady nodded.

Jim then also gave me the name Brian who had a link to Portugal. The lady confirmed that Brian was a nephew and a keen golfer who often went to Portugal to play.

'Jim can see him,' I told her. 'He says Brian needs to be careful of his diet. No butter, no full cream milk.'

She nodded. I was so pleased she had stood up. Jim was playing the role of guardian angel. He had been keeping his eye on his family from spirit and took the opportunity to speak to them and offer his concerns about how they were keeping.

Our souls are intrinsically linked to our bodies when we are alive so the healthier our bodies are, the more ability we have to nourish our souls. If we are healthy we can share and spread love and help our children develop their souls too. Being healthy aids happiness and happiness has a ripple effect, it spreads and that's what spirit wants.

When we do become unwell they come to us and care for us.

At a show on the south coast a lady took a message from a woman in spirit called Wendy.

'She was my best friend and she had a stroke,' the lady in the audience explained.

Wendy put words in my head. I got the name Mick.

'Who is Mick,' I asked.

'My partner who passed away,' the lady answered.

'She wants you to know she is with him and they are here for you.'

Then I felt a strange sensation down my right side. I asked the lady what it meant.

She explained that she had just been diagnosed with Parkinson's disease. The spirits were coming through for her to reassure her.

'They love you and they are taking care of you. They know what is going on and they will try and help you,' I said.

How can I lead a spiritual life?

If you are asking about being more religious, you are asking the wrong person. To me, being spiritual is something different to being religious. Being religious means following a set of rules laid down by someone. It means being observant and following a belief system. To be religious you have to follow certain practices and customs.

Being spiritual is different. Spirituality is about how you treat yourself and the world around you. It is about listening to yourself and your intuition. It is about loving and understanding. We should never be aware of leading a spiritual life. It is too pious. Anyone who is always thinking 'I need to lead a spiritual life' will probably never lead one. I liken it to going on a diet. If you make a big song and dance about it and tell everyone you are on one, the chances are you will fail. If you wake up one morning and make a personal decision to eat more healthily and exercise more you are more likely to lose weight. It is like that with spirituality.

Leading a spiritual life is a personal thing and it starts from within.

It is a moveable feast, unlike religion which is dogmatic and prescribed. Being spiritual doesn't have to mean you behave like a saint all the time because none of us are saints. Little things can be spiritual, like kindness, love, giving someone a hug or an encouraging word or going to visit an elderly relative.

Does my mum forgive me for putting her in a home?

As we have seen in earlier questions, sadly sometimes guilt and death go hand in hand. To us, death isn't always expected and when it comes suddenly we can be left with so many unresolved issues if we did not get the opportunity to say what we wanted to say to the deceased. We may have rowed before they died or we may have done something we feel guilty about and never had the chance to seek forgiveness.

Guilt and the desire for forgiveness are regular themes that appear through my work and one of the most common situations to generate these emotions is when a family has had to make the decision to place an ailing parent in a home.

In life we have to make hard choices. Sometimes we are placed in positions we wouldn't choose to be in and we have to do things we don't want to do. In an ideal world no one would want to put a loved one in a home when it is apparent that person is against the idea of going there. The world is not ideal however and this is a scenario increasing numbers of people face as the population becomes older and as modern medicine keeps people alive for longer, even after they have suffered debilitating events such as strokes and heart attacks. It is often impossible for people to care for their parents as they have careers and family and are not qualified to cope with the demands of an elderly person, especially someone with a condition such as dementia. In these cases it would be dangerous for the sufferer to live on their own. It is even more difficult when the parent doesn't want to leave their home. The guilt and the desire for forgiveness come about when the parent dies because inevitably, especially when dementia has been a factor, there has not been the opportunity to talk things through. Over the years I have dealt with this issue scores of times. People can torture themselves worrying about how their parent felt in their last days. Their souls know this and they come back to soothe fears. When spirits come back the slate is always wiped clean, even when they protested about the situation on Earth plane.

For example the spirit of Peter came into my head an hour and a half before I went on stage at a show in the north of England. He had been there, waiting patiently until the curtain went up. I could feel he was a kind man and he was quietly purposeful. He gave me the name Helen.

The message was taken by a woman in the front row. I could feel the energy glow as she stood up. There was no mistaking she was the intended recipient. She confirmed that Peter was in spirit and he had a daughter Helen.

He spoke to me and told me he was very tired towards the end of his.

'They kept giving me that stuff,' he sighed. 'It made me so tired.'

The people in the home looking after him had given him medication in his final days to control the pain he was in but it had made him unresponsive. His daughter had been wracked with guilt about this.

'There have been questions over whether he should have been given the medication,' I told the receiver. 'Helen feels terrible that he was given it but they had to allow him to have it so he could get through the day.

'He wants everyone to know that he is ok now, he is safe and there is no need to be guilty.'

Spirits do not like to see us suffer with guilt and they come back to make amends for many reasons.

One of the most heart-warming messages I have delivered in recent times happened in Devon. It started with a photograph of a boy. His mother had left it on stage and I picked it out at random and showed it to the audience. When she stood she was shaking. I knew the little boy was dead. He was with me on stage.

A sentence popped into my head.

'He's telling me that they don't live there anymore,' I explained.

Tears streamed down his mother's face.

'We moved house recently and I felt really guilty,' she said.

I tried my best to put her mind at rest.

'He knows,' I told her. 'He understands and he

wants you to know that wherever you go, he will be with you. He is in your heart. He is your whole life.'

The boy spoke again but I could barely make out his words.

'Is there someone called Zane,' I asked. 'Or maybe he's saying Seine... the river Seine. Did someone recently come back from Paris?'

The lady confirmed that her other son had just returned from a trip to Paris.

'He's trying to talk to me,' I said. 'He was on that trip with your son. He is trying to tell me he was there. He is with his brother. He is with all of you. He is participating in your lives.'

The woman smiled through her tears.

'His brother will be really pleased because the morning he died they had a really big argument and his brother can never get over the fact that...' she trailed off, lost in her grief.

'Unexpected sudden passings can leave so much guilt and that's not how it should be,' I said. 'He is talking to me and I don't feel that is right. You should be able to feel him too. If you take nothing else from this night know that your boy's soul is there with you.'

It is one of the aspects of my work that I feel guilty about. Why should I have the right to connect and feel the spirits of loved ones so intensely when their families can't. That's why I always encourage people to look for the signs and acknowledge them. As I get older it has become more of a dilemma. I look at my eight grandchildren and I think if anything happened to them what would I do? How much would I give just to feel them and speak to them?

Not being able to repent and say sorry can feel like a punishment. That privilege gets taken away from you by death and you feel the last emotions you exchanged with the deceased will be the ones that remain forever. In this case, as hard as it is, you need to step back and look at the big picture of the relationship you had with that person. If, on the whole it was loving, that love will remain. It will be what they carry over with them. You might have had an argument with someone before they died but that shouldn't affect how you felt and how they felt about you. You have to try and look at things logically, which is hard because logic goes out the window when you are grieving.

Another issue that brings guilty feelings is termination. Even babies that are just a few weeks old have souls and their energy feels pure and new. They are unencumbered by life and experience. Is it right to terminate them? I believe that women have to have a choice over their bodies and when they come through I never feel they are angry. They still have a loving bond to their mother.

Guilt is a huge part of any loss. It is probably the biggest reason why people come and see me. Guilt is there with every passing. I say to people never feel that it is too late. Yes the physical body isn't there but the soul is and it is there with you.

You can pull on their soul and even though you may have had a difficult relationship in life, you can still make amends. You can talk to a loved one from the moment they pass. You can still be in touch. You don't need a medium, you can make contact through your own psychic inner core. What you need to remember is that in life it is human to have ups and downs in all relationships. How many times have we all had a row with someone and walked out without resolving the issue? In the very times when that happens and someone dies the cost and the guilt can be overwhelming. As can the anger; why did he storm out? You immediately think the last thing the dead person remembered was the row and the conflict. It is not. They understand and they don't want us to feel guilty. Spirits come through to me and they say that all the time.

How long after we die can we come through as a spirit?

There are no hard and fast rules. It depends on the individual spirit and the circumstances. I have had people who have come through on the day of their funeral and others who have waited 70 years. To a large degree it is about accessing the appropriate medium. If someone dies and there is someone there who can take the message effectively, they can come through immediately after passing. I guess it's like making a call before the days of mobile phones. You could only get your message across if you were near a phone box and that phone box had to be working and you needed to have the right change.

To spirits the time gap doesn't matter because there is no time on the other side. They do not feel time. We made the clock on Earth plane because we have night and day and needed a time system to map our limited lifespan. Their world is eternal.

Recent passings can often feel different when they come through, almost as if they are feeling their way. In one recent reading a recently passed spirit opened the door for another.

The name that came through was Terry.

'If you don't get that tax sorted, God help you,'

was his message. I could see him. He was a hand-some man in his sixties. He was worried about finances.

'You can't fiddle the books,' he was telling me. I could feel his anxiety. I also got the name Jan or Janet. He showed me the scene of his funeral. There were so many mourners and he was amazed at all the flowers. He had been trying to get through to me for several hours.

'He wants to help his family. I feel there are people who are struggling to cope with this man's death. It feels very recent,' I told the audience.

I got the names Nick and Alan. There was a lot of information. He died of cancer and there was a pain in his bones, especially in his back.

Initially no one took the message but I knew that it was meant for someone out in the auditorium. It was too clear.

Eventually a lady stood up.

'What is it that makes sense to you?' I asked.

'My name is Terri,' she said. 'I run a family busi-ness. There is a Nick and an Alan in my family.' But I had the feeling that the message wasn't for her. I would never make a message fit and I apologised to her and moved on.

I was about to focus on another message when the man in spirit gave me the name Janet. It came through loud and clear and he refused to make way for another spirit. He was blocking my mind.

'I know there is someone here who knows this person and whatever your reasons for not standing

I understand, but this opportunity will not come again so please don't be nervous,' I said.

A hand rose tentatively from the seats at the side of the stage. The name Janet came through again, even clearer.

'Are you Janet,' I asked.

The lady who had raised her hand nodded.

I tried to calm her nerves.

'It's very good of you to stand up. I realise you were reticent so thank you,' I soothed.

'He only passed on Sunday,' she said quietly. She was shaking. The death had only happened three days before. 'His name was Terry, he had bone cancer. The family are all having a hard time at the moment because of the tax affairs and the will.'

The next spirit to come through was a lady called June. She had been poorly for many years and had become increasingly weaker. She wanted to talk to someone called Karen. She explained how she fought her illness but was never able to recover. A lady stood.

'I went to June's funeral last week, she was my mum's best friend. They had known each other since they were children.'

'Another one!' I gasped. There is always a link, a hook between the messages and June had come through because her death was so recent, just like Terry's.

'There is always a hook from a previous message,' I said.

The lady continued.

'She had been ill for years and I am Karen.'

Death certainly isn't the end. I've even come across the spirits of people who have 'grown' after death. I do not know why it happens but in some cases, especially when it is a child who has passed, when they come through to me they can appear older than they were when they died. Often this spiritual ageing process seems to stop when someone else close to them dies. For example at a show in Aberdeen I picked up the spirit of a little girl. Immediately I was overcome by the feeling of heat. I got her name and her father took the message and explained that she had died tragically after being scalded in the bath. When she appeared to me she looked around six years of age. Her father told me she had died when she was two. Then I saw her standing with another lady whose name was Rose. The man explained that Rose was his mother, the girl's gran, and that Rose had died four years after her granddaughter, when she would have been six. I was as if the little girl had grown before she was joined by her gran.

If I don't believe
will I still have an afterlife?

You're in luck! You will. What I do is not about a faith system or a religion and you don't have to be a believer. There is always every form of denomination in my audience and spirit comes through no matter what the receiver believes in. Each faith system says the only way you can know the afterlife is by following its own specific set of rules but the reality is it is about trusting. When I give messages and deliver them without doubt, the spirits know I trust them and they give me more details. It works for everyone, no matter what. If, for example, you hear a song that reminds you of a departed loved one on the anniversary of their death, trust that you are being given a sign. When you place that trust in those circumstances, the spirit that gave you the sign will recognise that and give you more signs. If you put it down to coincidence the door will shut and you will not be given another sign.

Whatever we do or don't believe in, our soul or spirit lives on. You don't have to believe in a specific set of rules for that to happen because it is the natural order of things. It is what happens to us, whether we have followed one set of beliefs or another. It will still happen, your soul will still live

on no matter whether you believed in God, Allah,
Buddha or The Force from Star Wars.

What happens to spirits from thousands of years ago?

Spirits come through to us on Earth plane for a reason and the vast majority of times that reason is so they can connect to loved ones. Therefore if their loved ones are no longer here there is little reason for them to come back unless perhaps they have some unfinished business to attend too. People in spirit with no direct links to living people (everyone who dies leaves some link no matter how indirect) have less attachment to the physical realm. Instead they are in the afterlife with the souls of their loved ones. As generations pass, spirits have less cause to connect with our world, ones from hundreds and thousands of years ago are still there in the afterlife but have no reason to come through.

The exception to this rule is when someone on Earth plane begins to investigate their family tree because suddenly they are thought of. Memories will link them to us. Their names will be spoken and that process has the effect of drawing them to us. Some will be drawn to Earth plane by curiosity.

It is now easier than ever to research family trees thanks to the internet. Genealogy, boosted in popularity by TV shows such as Who Do You Think You Are, has become a common pastime.

And because of this I have noticed a trend of more 'old' spirits returning,

For example I was visited by one at a show in the North West.

I was scanning the audience and my eyes were drawn to a lady dressed in purple. I looked at her and I knew her name.

'Cheryl?'

She smiled and stood. I had someone in spirit, clear as a bell. Her name was Kitty.

'My great great great grandmother was Kitty,' she offered. We were going back a long way.

'I don't usually go back that far,' I explained. 'Have you been doing a family tree? Because there will be a reason why she's come through.'

'My aunt has,' Cheryl confirmed.

Kitty, who would never have met her in life, was linked to her through family and was coming through loud and clear, having been dead a long, long time, to tell her that everything was going to be ok.

Is the afterlife different for people who take their own lives?

Unless you are a truly evil person the afterlife is the same for us all. It is a wonderful place, full of love and peace. The way we die does little to alter that. Certain religions would lead you to think differently. In some, suicide is a sin and those who take their lives burn in Hell. I don't believe this is true. The only Hell is the one faced by loved ones left on Earth as they try to work out why that person took such drastic final action and whether there had been anything they could have done to change events.

Suicide is very common. They come through to me every night, mainly they are young men. Inevitably they want to reassure those they left behind.

While the question left on our lips when someone passes is usually 'why', I believe that it is always part of the plan. None of us go before we are meant to and suicide is just another way for us to pass into spirit. It becomes an issue for us because as human beings we are supposed to value life above all else and it seems unnatural for anyone to die by their own hands. Certain belief systems find it abhorrent and most people cannot fathom a situation where the best option appears to be death unless that situation means someone is suffering intolerable pain. But those who take their lives are often not in a rational place, unless they die through assisted suicide where their motives are usually medical. In most suicides emotions overpower the rational minds.

When they come through they try and explain this.

The spirit of a man who took his life appeared at a recent show. It was a heart-wrenching reading.

He wanted to connect with his daughter in the audience.

'I have your dad here for you,' I told her.

The girl was clearly emotional. She had lost her father in the most painful of circumstances. He had taken his own life. The validation was crystal clear. The details the spirit of her father had given were incredibly specific. There was a truck that he drove and a collection of personal belongings that he took with him when he took his life.

He showed me a tragic scene several days before his death. He had tried to kill himself before but did not succeed. He tried to hang himself at the bottom of a staircase.

The girl nodded.

'We lived in a pub and had a cellar, it happened there.'

'I have your dad here, he is showing me a scene. He couldn't cope, he was under so much pressure.'

He told me the address of his mother, who he visited often. Then he gave me his name: John.

His daughter confirmed all the details. She had obviously suffered great grief from his death but the reading hopefully gave her some peace. It was so exact that she could be left with no doubt that her father was finally at rest and was also with her in spirit.

Suicide leaves so many questions. Even if the person leaves a note it still seems inexplicable that our loved ones could resort to such measures. This is because, on the whole, suicide is a secretive moment. It is a singular pact between that person and their thoughts. It will never be totally explainable to those who are left. There is confusion, huge guilt and sometimes denial, like with a spirit called Rachel who had died just two weeks before she came through during a show in the north of England. She had hung herself in her home. Her mother was also in spirit. Rachel was showing me a scene; a copse of trees swaying in the wind. I described what I was seeing and the lady receiving the message confirmed that the scene sounded like Rachel's' mother's house, where her ashes had been taken just the previous day.

Rachel was telling me that she looked up at the trees. Then she mentioned something very uncomfortable.

I tried to be tactful to the lady I was relaying the message to.

'Does Rachel have a stepfather?' I asked.

The lady nodded.

'Do you know if he teased her about her sexuality or sex? That's why she did it,' I revealed.

The lady denied this. She told me that she knew

the family very well and that was not the reason Rachel had done what she had done.

It was a very awkward moment. I tried to explain that I respected them the same way that I respected everyone in the audience but that I also had to respect the spirits. And it was Rachel who was telling me these details.

The validation continued. She took me into a basement where she found solace and comfort. There was man there with her. He was harmless, he never did anything wrong but he was an alcoholic. He understood her. She used to go there.

The lady explained that she now lived in Rachel's house where there was a cellar where Rachel used to hold parties. She had a friend who lived next door and used to listen to her.

It was an incredible message. Poor Rachel, she just couldn't cope with her life. But I tried to explain that there is no shame in dying. Rachel suffered in life but in death she was in peace and she was where every other spirit resides.

It can also be very hard for the bereaved to accept that their loved ones desired death.

Lee came to me in spirit having taken his life. He had troubles from the age of eight. A lady took the message. I told her straight away.

'There is no shame in dying. I deal with so many suicides and they leave so many questions and so many mixed feelings. The biggest one is guilt. They are not well. They have this tsunami of emotion that wipes everything out.'

Everyone of us has those waves of emotion; including me. The times when you think you cannot take it anymore. But most of us are lucky and we have people around us who support us and that wave passes. But occasionally there are people who have nothing to hold on top, nothing to anchor them to the living world and they take their own lives. This was what Lee had done.

'He wants you to know he is safe,' I told her. 'I can't lie. He also wants you to know that he is happy where he is. This is what he wanted.'

But other times there are tragedies when desperate people do not mean to take their lives. We call it a cry for help. When these cries go unheard and the person dies it can be the cruellest death of all.

These spirits also come through to reassure their loved ones.

At a show in Wales, as I began the evening, I sensed a girl standing on the stage to the side of me. I could see her clearly in my mind's eye. Her head was bowed. She seemed shy. I wanted to draw her out from the side of the stage and in my head I told her everything was okay and that she should point out who she wanted to give her message to. She told me her name was Cara, that she was 24 and then she put her head in her hands. I sensed she was in pain and also in distress in her final moments.

A woman in the audience stood to take the message and confirmed that a friend of her daughter's was named Cara and that three weeks previously, at the age of 24, she had taken her own life by overdosing on pills.

'I am sorry, I didn't mean it,' were the words Cara wanted me to relay.

She really didn't mean to do it and the woman confirmed that many people who knew her shared the same suspicions.

Was it an accident? On Earth plane it was but Cara's death was planned for her by a higher power. For her loved ones left here it was no consolation but she went when she was meant to go.

Will my dead husband mind if I remarry?

Love works differently on Earth plane and in the afterlife when it comes to our intimate relationships. Here, the love we have with our boyfriends, girlfriends, husbands and wives is exclusive. On the whole we have one partner at a time and it is common to settle down with just one person. Monogamy is the general rule unless you are unfaithful or a swinger! I am devoted to John and he is devoted to me and that excludes all others. It is a lovely way to be and for most that arrangement feels right.

In spirit however, love is inclusive. Everyone is drawn into each other's loving energy. Don't get the wrong idea. There is nothing seedy about it. The love that binds spirit energy is a pure love and the reason we are inclusive but spirit is exclusive boils down to our bodies. Flesh and blood comes with certain urges and needs. I'm not just talking about sexual desire. We also have a need to be loved which doesn't translate in spirit world. There are no needs or urges there, love is everything and all around.

In the vast majority of cases where a spirit has come through and registered that a widow has moved on with a new lover, the energy is accepting and encouraging. Often they joke about the situation.

Sometimes however it's not always the love that passes over. Negative feelings and emotions are displayed on rare occasions as a reminder but I always get the impression they do not really matter. Sometimes a spirit will use them to make a specific point. For example I picked up the energy of a recently departed young woman at a show in Leeds. It came from a photograph someone had left. When I picked it out I realised I had seen the girl on stage earlier in the evening. The lady who left it told me she had died a couple of days previously and she was a next door neighbour. There was slight confusion in the message to begin with as I heard a deep voice and got the sensation that my throat was tightening. The lady who had left the picture confirmed that she had also put another photo in the tray of a friend who had hung himself. Both spirits were on stage, superimposed on one another.

'This is very specific,' I told the lady in the audience. 'Did someone take steroids?'

She nodded.

'Yes, her ex-husband.'

'She's not been buried yet, she doesn't want him at the funeral,' I continued. 'It's because of the steroids. She knows he'll be spaced out.'

She was adamant. I could tell from her energy that there was no love lost between her and her ex and she felt strongly about not having him there. It is rare to feel hate in a reading and although there was a strong message of disapproval, I got the impression that she did not want him to stay away from her funeral because they did not get on when she was alive, she wanted him to stay away to protect the other guests. Ultimately spirits want their loved ones to be happy.

Can my gran see me having sex from the afterlife?

In short, yes she can! But before you join a monastic order and renounce any temptations of the flesh bear in mind that she probably won't want too, and even if she did, from a spiritual perspective it really wouldn't bother her as much as it bothers you. In fact the only time she'd be likely to intervene or show any interest in any way in your intimate life would be if you were in danger or if your health was at risk in any way. If this were the case she would send you a sign, rather than barge in and interrupt you.

It is true that our loved ones are always with us. They reside in our thoughts and in our hearts and we bring them too us with thoughts and dreams. So as long as you don't think about your gran while you are having a bit of nookie, she's unlikely to make her presence known.

The pleasure we receive through physical contact on Earth plane is by its very nature related to the physical body. And because of that, those feelings we have stay on Earth plane and do not translate into the afterlife. So while love is what draws spirits to us, physical attraction, lust, call it what you will, is bound up with the body and isn't something that spirits are concerned with. When we have a deep spiritual connection to someone and we love them dearly we call them our soulmate because they touch our souls, not just our bodies.

It can be quite disconcerting to think that our loved ones are with us all the time. Sometimes we do things that we wouldn't want other people to see or to know about, but spirits understand that none of us are born with a halo over our head. We all err sometimes; it is part of being human. When we do they keep an eye on us but they rarely intervene and they do not judge.

There have been occasions during shows when spirits have mentioned things to me which I know will be embarrassing for the receiver. These situations always present me with a moral dilemma. Should I say something or keep quiet? Ultimately I have to be faithful to the message and so I often have to be tactful in the way I deliver the information.

For example at one show in the North West I was relaying a message from a father in spirit to his son in the audience. Every detail had been correct and as I was discussing the father's concerns about his son's health I began to smell a pungent aroma in stage. I grew up in the sixties so I vaguely recognised what it was!

"He's telling you to lay off the… errr," I didn't know how to diplomatic so I mimed taking a draw on a cigarette.

The young man in the audience laughed nervously.

"He knows you do it but he says you need to watch your chest. It's not doing you any good in the long run," I explained.

There are other times when a spirit will use an indiscretion as a joke, to make a receiver feel better about a situation and to let them know that they need not worry.

How do you communicate with spirits who don't speak English?

I interpret the energy. I am not hearing sounds, I am reading energy, and the energy transcends language. I interpret what I get in my head into English words because English is the language I speak. That is my theory anyway and it must be right because I can't speak any other language except for English but during my life I have taken messages from people who speak all different types of languages. It never usually presents a problem, except sometimes with names. For example I was performing at a show in Leeds when a lady from the Czech Republic took a message. I could understand what the spirit was telling me but I had trouble deciphering her accent. I had the name Joseph and the word 'pepper'. The lady explained that her grandfather was called Joseph but his nickname was 'Pepper'. I also got the name Tina. She explained that her grandmother, also in spirit, was very short and that her nickname translated into the English word 'tiny'.

At one reading in Australia the word for grandmother came through but I was hearing it in Maltese. I repeated what I was hearing in my mind. It made no sense to me at all until the lady who had taken the message explained to me that her

Gran had been born in Malta and lived there for much of her life. When I pick up on a message I say exactly what I hear in my head and that's how I get my 'hits'. I never self-edit because they are giving me the signs and that is what they want me to say. Sometimes I'll think to myself I can't say that, but I have to trust what comes into my head, no matter how silly I might sound.

I will pick up terms and ways of explaining things that have cultural differences depending on where the spirit came from and how he or she spoke when they were alive. Their vocabulary was part of their personality and is another way to identify them. Most people have habits in their speech, they may say 'innit' at the end of the sentence. These idiosyncrasies come across when they make contact.

What's it like being Sally Morgan

One of the most common questions I get asked is: 'what's it like being you'. I can understand why people are fascinated. Let's face it; I am a curiosity. I'm a normal mother and grandmother with an amazing gift. I talk to dead people! Just by admitting that leaves me open to criticism and curiosity. I'm glad people ask and I'm glad people want to understand.

The short answer to the question is that when I am in full swing in the throes of a national tour my life becomes surreal. It feels as though I am living someone else's life (often I am living lots of people's lives through messages on stage). I'm sure it would eventually send me doolally if I didn't have the influence of John. He doesn't realise it but he is very grounding. I know I couldn't operate at the level I do if I didn't have him and the support of my family.

It's a hectic, mad world. When you are well-known you are wide open. I am not complaining. I chose to take my gift to a larger audience and by doing that I stuck my head above the parapet. Some days I put on my helmet and dodge the bullets but on the whole I know I am incredibly privileged to do the work I do and there is far more smooth than rough.

The mechanics of what I do are simple. I get thoughts. They are not my thoughts. They are thoughts from spirit. It usually starts with a name. I will walk out on stage and think "oh goodness me, is your name Tony?" And then I'll get more, I may see how Tony died, maybe Tony was run over by a car and I'll get the make and model of the car. It usually starts with the death; how it occurred, where it occurred, who else was involved. Unfortunately this can sometimes be very traumatic if, for example, the death was a murder. It may sound like a callous way to introduce a spirit to a loved one but each death is a fingerprint and the details help to identify the person in spirit. I get given enough information to narrow down the identity of the person in spirit. I might get two people who have died from a heart attack on the 10th of Dec at 6pm who are both called Derek but there will be something unique about each death. Maybe one Derek died in a blue sweater. It can be as simple as that. There is always a way spirit can eliminate other possibilities.

The details can be incredibly detailed. For example at a show in Australia I was shown details of a man who hung himself. I was in a garage and I could see a young man standing on the roof of a small green car parked there. He was jumping on the roof. Next I saw him lying dead on the bonnet, suspended by a rope round his neck with one leg on the roof. He had tried to climb back up as he was being strangled. He showed me that because it was unique. People die by similar methods but there will always be a unique element. That boy had died quite slowly. Although it is hard to hear details that sound gruesome in the cold light of day, when I am talking through messages at a show in the right context it isn't gruesome.

Often they queue, like at the deli counter in the supermarket. They line up in my head. I can see them come in and go back and come in again, all waiting their turn. They are waiting for someone in the audience to say "yes, that's for me". Sometimes however there will be ones that grab my attention. It may not seem fair to people who are desperate for a message but I am only human. I don't know how to filter messages and I don't think I am supposed too. If they can distract me enough, if they can show me something gruesome, it gets my attention even though as I get older I find it more difficult to look at these gruesome things.

I see these details as if they are being described to me by thought. I can also see literally, as if there is someone next to me, someone solid. A lot of people would say a ghost or a presence or entity or vision, mainly I see in my mind's eye. Spirits talk to me but not in the way we talk to our friends. The speech comes to me in a thought process which is so deeply ingrained in my own thought process that in part I become the person I am connected with. I pick up their vocabulary and mannerisms. Some would say I become possessed which is an understandable assumption to make but I would say it is more that I am in tune with their energy; their being.

When I am away from home and doing a show I can wake in the hotel in the morning and think about the show that night and I start getting messages. It can be all day sometimes. I look at a message like a puzzle. You cannot force pieces in otherwise the whole thing will kink and you won't be able to finish it.

There is no doubt about it that in the last three years certain aspects of my ability have altered. My psychic cells have discovered new pathways to link more closely to spirit, which is why I can take on the literal presence of a person. I can stand like them and adopt their gait. I also feel their pain, which is an unpleasant side effect. Recently a murder victim came through who had his throat slashed. All of a sudden I felt their pain. It was horrendous and at times like those I have to remind myself that what I am feeling is not real, it's a projection of what they felt. I use my psychic muscle intensely. I am like an Olympic athlete when it comes to psychic ability. I could be in Team GB if there was a psychic event. The whole process is fuelled by energy which comes from spirit world and from the public.

There is a huge responsibility in my work. It is so difficult for me because I cannot bring them back. I find it very hard sometimes. The one comfort I have is the comfort of knowing that the messages I receive do in many ways make things easier for the people left behind, they offer comfort, conclusions, love, answers. I cannot ever know other people's grief because grief is such a personal thing. The moment a loved one dies, lives are changed forever. They are never the same again. I hope that from the evenings I do people are able to take on board the possibility that they can reach out to those they have lost. I am a pleaser, I never want to hurt or offend anyone. I am hypersensitive as a medium to people's feelings but am very aware my pact is with spirit. This means that I have to pass on messages as truthfully and as clearly as I can from the information I am picking up and hopefully if my work changes someone's life it is for the better. I know I give people comfort because over the years I have been told by thousands of people.

It is not magic, I am not playing tricks with people, I am not clever enough. I am not a psychologist or a psychiatrist. I don't know how to perform mind tricks. I am Sally Morgan, a very ordinary woman who has opened up something in her mind and can see and hear things and receive messages from people that are no longer alive. Modern legislation insists that when I go on stage it is very important that the name entertainment should be included in what I do. I don't mind. It's a fact of life. I can be entertaining. I have a wicked sense of humour and I hope people enjoy coming to my shows. If they didn't I wouldn't be able to work as hard as I do. I have to look at it as being just a word to allow me to do what I do.

Most religions and people who practice things that others have trouble accepting have gone through phases of being forced underground.

There are days when I wake and am frightened about what may lay ahead for me because of my work. I worry on a personal level about letting people down. There are huge expectations from people which I totally understand. I can put myself in their shoes and see why they have these expectations. I get up in the morning because of this. I want to help and I want to make people realise there is hope. Of course there have been times when I have wanted the world to go away. I have run the gauntlet most of my life.

My family keeps me grounded. As soon as I finish work and set foot over the threshold I am Sally or Mum. It can't be any other way because I have to be me to be able to do this extraordinary job. When I am not working I am just Sal. I have a lot of good friends and a lovely family.

I don't know how long I can sustain doing what I do. I am certainly not thinking about retirement. I know the ability I have improves with age which is completely at odds with everything else in life. I believe it is organic and it grows with me and evolves and changes. It moves forward and to the side and finds new pathways, it brings experiences into my life on a personal level and has introduced me to people and situations I could have only dreamed about so I am not complaining. If am lucky to be doing this when I am 70 I will be better than I am today. I love what I do. I'll retire the day I wake up and think I don't want to do this or when the public decides to stop coming to see me.

There are a lot of different things happening in my world and my work. Although the shows will continue in the same vein, I am investigating new areas. Maybe my dream of having a Psychic Centre of some sort may happen. My work is vocational, I can never retire. It goes with me to the grave.

I like to think that I have dragged mediumship into the 21st century and hopefully I haven't demeaned it.

Epilogue
Australia: July 2013

The miles dropped away and as they did I could feel myself start to relax. The further from the UK we got, the further away the last two years felt. My shoulders dropped and I sunk back further into the seat as the jet flew out over the south coast and across to Europe. I had done what I set out to do. I had cleared my name.

It was going to be a long flight and I closed my eyes and let peaceful sleep creep over me.

The last few weeks had been a blur. The legal case was over and I was on the way to Australia for a series of shows. It was new beginning for me and couldn't have come at a better time. I'd never toured extensively in a foreign country and it felt right to put some distance between myself and the UK. I was wary at home. I'd been stung and despite the apology I received, I worried what people thought of me. Australia offered something new. I hadn't planned for the tour to coincide with the end of my legal case, I believe that was the way spirit orchestrated it.

I must have been exhausted because I slept for most of the first stage of the flight. The tour was going to be gruelling. We had booked in as many dates as we could over a five week period covering most of the large cities in the country. The distances between each were vast and I would be spending more time travelling on the road and in the air than I would be stationary. But I didn't care. It was a chance to test new waters and see how I would be received in a new country. I was excited but apprehensive.

I needn't have worried. The reception I got was warm and welcoming. People were genuinely interested in my work and the venues started to fill up as locals and ex pats alike began to buy tickets to find out who this strange woman from the UK who claimed she could talk to the dead was.

And that's when I began to notice the energy. The more shows I did, the purer the energy felt. I couldn't quite put my finger on it at first but then it started to make sense. The country was open. It felt like it accepted me and who I was. Sure, there were people who would raise an eyebrow and question whether I was for real. But they far outweighed the people who took the attitude of "ok, let's see what you can do". I wasn't discounted straight away. Even the cynics were willing to listen and to be open-minded. I found it very refreshing and it affected the shows. People started to trust and the more they started to trust, the more hits came through.

Some amazing things happened.

In a place called Bankstown I sensed the spirit of a young girl. As her image materialised in my mind's eye my blood ran cold. She was stooped and her face was directed away from me but even from my obscured viewpoint I could see the burns all over her body. I got the name Connie.

'I'm looking at something that isn't very nice,' I told the audience. 'Normally when I have something heavy I prefer to deal with it in the second half.' It was early in the show and I usually like to ease people in gently! But Connie would not go away.

'Her name is Connie. There were very bad burns on her. Her hair and neck area were in fire.'

I could hear the noise of something popping. Then I felt the sensation of falling from a great height.

The energy felt so strong I knew the massage was meant for someone. I also got the name Ginger.

A lady took the message and explained that she had a friend who was recently murdered and her body had been set alight. But the names did not match. As much as I would have liked to have given her the message I knew it wasn't for her. The details did not match. I sensed that when Connie died there were other people present. Sadly no one else took the message and I moved on.

Then in the interval something strange happened. Two girls approached one of my staff in the foyer and told her that a year ago there had been a house fire a few blocks away from the theatre. Two girls had died in it. Their names were Connie and Ginger. The girls said they didn't take the message because they assumed it was meant for someone else. I heard about this just before I took to the stage for the second half of the show. I could have mentioned it but I didn't for two reasons. Firstly once the message has gone it has gone. Connie's spirit had left. I do not force spirit through and I wasn't prepared to try. That is why I am always so adamant about people taking messages. You only get one shot and it is such a rare privilege. The second reason I decided to stay silent had much to do with the battering I had received over the newspaper articles. I simply didn't want people to think that I had gone off at the interval and Googled details about local tragedies.

At every show there were streams of amazing messages. A few days later I was on stage in a place called Penrith when another young girl came through. I could feel her and the panic she felt at the end of her life. She was saying what sounded like "Orla" and I could feel that there had been something wrong with her arms. She was 11 when she died.

I tried to work out what was wrong with her arms. It felt as though they were being pulled back and they felt heavy. Perhaps they had been in plaster?

Then I felt water rising up. As the details were coming through I recounted them to the audience and a lady sitting near the back raised her arm.

'I don't like what I am seeing. Was she caught under her right arm? Was that how she died?'

The voice in my head became clearer.

'I think she is saying 'all over',' I explained.

The lady stood.

'It's not a nice story,' she said. 'She was raped and murdered and put in a pond with rocks in her backpack.'

Her arms were being pulled back by the weight of the rocks pulling her down.

'When she was put in that pond she was dead,' I explained. 'She is safe now.'

Show after show the spirits came pouring through with amazingly accurate information. At another show in a place called Juniors I picked up the energy of man before I went on stage. I was sitting quietly in my changing room when he hijacked my thoughts. The words in my mind were foreign. "Givan... Givan..."

I also felt there had been a birth in the family.

I explained this to the audience and pointed out where in the audience he was looking. A lady stood immediately with a younger woman. I had been pointing directly at them.

'What have I said that makes sense to you?' I asked.

'My name is Givan, my father has passed and my daughter has had a little baby girl,' she said. The audience cheered (the Aussies were very enthusiastic).

'He's not talking English,' I said. The lady nodded.

The man in spirit showed me a scene of the baby in a lovely frilly dress and gave me the name Chris.

I told the woman and tearfully she explained that her daughter's name was Christine.

'He's been there with them,' I explained.

The man went on to explain that Christine should be careful of her back and also that his daughter Rose should be careful of her head. He was keeping an eye on them from spirit. The energy was linked and I felt locked in to the message.

I ended the message and the ladies sat down.

The next spirit came through immediately. His name was Steve and he had died in an accident. There had been a huge compensation claim connected to his death.

The same lady stood again. 'My cousin was Steve and he died when he was hit by a train. His family were awarded compensation for it.'

It was an amazing double! The energy from the first spirit was so strong it had hooked in Steve's spirit as well.

As the tour progressed I could feel all my confidence coming back to me. The more confident I was, the more messages I passed on. It was an amazing five weeks but perhaps the high point was when I was invited on a national television show to talk about my work.

I won't lie, I was a little concerned at first. I have appeared on shows in the UK before and been hijacked by sceptical attitudes. The show in Australia was called The Daily Edition. I settled into the seat ready to be interviewed by host Tom Williams and as soon as he introduced himself I felt at ease because I could tell he had no other agenda other than to find out about me.

He was curious but he was open. And because of that I started to pick up information about him. For a moment I was confused. Spirit was showing me something that I knew was a closely guarded secret. Was I supposed to say something?

Then Tom gave me the opportunity.

'Are you picking up anything about the presenters,' he asked.

I took a breath. I was certain what I was about to say was the truth but if he denied it I would look like a fool, and worse, a liar.

'There is a child on the way for you.'

Tom was dumbstruck, while his co presenters looked on mutely he confirmed that his wife was expecting. He explained to his emotional colleagues that he was going to break the news later in the week and that him and his wife had been trying for quite a while as most of the other people on the show had children and he was beginning to feel left out.

Everyone in the studio was emotional and it became even more amazing when I told Tom's co-host, Sally Obermeder, that she would adopt a child in the future. She explained that she had survived cancer and that had made it risky for her to conceive so she had been discussing adoption.

The show was live and by the following day the news of my accuracy had spread across Australia and subsequently the world. In a weird stroke of irony, one of the news outlets in the UK that covered the story was none other than the Daily Mail!

Australia was cleansing for me. All the worries and fears I had were washed away and when I returned I was physically tired from all the travelling but mentally and spiritually reinvigorated. Spirit had been there when I needed it most. They were literally swarming around me at each venue making sure the word of my genuine ability got out. And when I most needed them on national television they were there for me again.

They can be there for you too. Life is full of trials and it's not easy. Along the way we face hardship, pain and loss. That is fact. But there are always people there to support and guide us. Often we don't see them. Sometimes we have to throw caution to the wind and trust that they are there and that the signs they send us are real. And if we trust and we open ourselves to possibility we will never be alone.

Acknowledgements

Thank you to Nick Harding for all his hard work and meticulous research. Thanks to Hayley, Sara and the team at SMHQ for their dedication to excellence. And last but not least (I know he always seems to be at the end), the one and only John Morgan, my husband, for making me endless cups of tea, listening to paragraph after paragraph and encouraging me to keep going.

Organisations & Charities

Listed below are details for both organisations and charities that deal with everything from the practicalities of what to do when a passing occurs to offering advice and guidance through difficult situations. There are lots of people out there who can assist and support you when you need it most.

Bearevement

Counselling Directory
www.counselling-directory.org.uk

Bereavement Advice Centre
www.bereavementadvice.org

British Association for Counselling and Psychotherapy
www.bacp.co.uk

Cruse Bereavement Care
www.crusebereavementcare.org.uk

Depression Alliance
www.depressionalliance.org

RoadPeace – supporting road traffic victims & their families
www.roadpeace.org

National Association of Widows
www.nawidows.org.uk/

Samaritans
www.samaritans.org

Support After Murder and Manslaughter
www.samm.org.uk

Funerals, memorials, practicalities

Memorial Awareness Board
www.namm.org.uk

National Association of Funeral Directors
www.nafd.org.uk

Woodland Trust Legacies – Assisstance in making a will and leaving
a legacy
www.woodlandtrust.org.uk

Terminal illness, hospices, palliative care

ACT – Help for families caring for children with life-threatening or
terminal conditions.
www.act.org.uk

Association of Children's Hospices
www.childhospice.org.uk

Growth House
www.growthhouse.org

Help the Hospices
www.helpthehospices.org.uk

Macmillan Cancer Support
www.macmillan.org.uk

Supporting bereaved children and young people

Jigsaw4U – Charity who look after children and young people through trauma, loss and bereavement.
www.jigsaw4u.org.uk

The Child Bereavement Trust
www.childbereavement.org.uk

ChildLine
www.childline.org.uk

Grief Encounter – Counselling for bereaved children and teenages.
www.griefencounter.org.uk

Support For Carers

Carers UK
www.carersuk.org

When a baby or child passes

The Child Bereavement Trust
www.childbereavement.org.uk

The Compassionate Friends – Support for bereaved parents and their families.
www.tcf.org.uk

SANDS – Stillbirth and Neonatal Death Society
www.uk-sands.org

Loss in pregnancy

Miscarriage Association
www.miscarriageassociation.org.uk

Parentsplace.com
www.ivillage.com

MY PSYCHIC LIFE

Sally Morgan has been psychic since she can remember. She saw her first ghost at the age of four and has been speaking to spirits and passing on their messages, hopes and fears to the living with astonishing accuracy for decades.

Sally's remarkable story recounts the first-hand experiences of intense conflict and personal turmoil which helped her understand her amazing ability and become a professional medium. She has now given thousands of readings for people who have experienced personal tragedy or suffered great loss. Packed with amazing anecdotes that will send a shiver down the spine, this is Sally's remarkable story.

Buy online – www.sallymorgan.tv

SALLY MORGAN

Healing Spirits

How the Other Side can help your grieving heart

BY THE AUTHOR OF THE *SUNDAY TIMES* BESTSELLER *MY PSYCHIC LIFE*

HEALING
SPIRITS

When loved ones die, where do they go? Are they still with us? Can they see and hear us?

In this book Sally Morgan, the country's much-loved psychic, explores the process of passing over and the earth-shattering feelings that come from losing someone close to us. She paints an enormously reassuring picture of the afterlife, drawing draws from her own experience, as well as from the hundreds of people she has helped over the years. Ultimately, this is a wonderfully uplifting book. Sally brings us closer to her universe and shows us that we too can listen to the spirit world.

Packed with amazing anecdotes and fascinating insights, Healing Spirits is an unforgettable journey with an inspiring guide.

Buy online – www.sallymorgan.tv

SALLY MORGAN

Life After Death

Messages of Love from the Other Side

BY THE AUTHOR OF THE *SUNDAY TIMES* BESTSELLER, *MY PSYCHIC LIFE*

LIFE AFTER DEATH

Travelling around the country for her hit TV show, Psychic Sally: On the Road, Sally Morgan delivers messages of comfort from beyond the grave to her stunned audiences. In Life After Death she takes the reader on the road with her and details the hair-raising events she witnesses. Read about the two women whose dead babies found each other in the spirit world, the father in row E whose killer son pleaded for forgiveness and the woman whose ten-year-old daughter had died in a tragic accident and wanted to let her mummy know she was no longer in pain.

Thanks to her incredible powers, Sally reveals secrets from the afterlife and helps people cope with the loss of loved ones.

Buy online – www.sallymorgan.tv